ACT JUSTLY,
LOVE TENDERLY

*Lifelong Lessons
in Conscience and Calling*

John Neafsey

ORBIS BOOKS

Maryknoll, New York 10545

Founded in 1970, Orbis Books endeavors to publish works that enlighten the mind, nourish the spirit, and challenge the conscience. The publishing arm of the Maryknoll Fathers and Brothers, Orbis seeks to explore the global dimensions of the Christian faith and mission, to invite dialogue with diverse cultures and religious traditions, and to serve the cause of reconciliation and peace. The books published reflect the views of their authors and do not represent the official position of the Maryknoll Society. To learn more about Maryknoll and Orbis Books, please visit our website at www.maryknollsociety.org.

Copyright ©2016 by John Neafsey.
Published by Orbis Books, Box 302, Maryknoll, NY 10545-0302.
All rights reserved.
No part of this publication may be reproduced or transmitted in any form or by any means, electronic or mechanical, including photocopying, recording, or any information storage or retrieval system, without prior permission in writing from the publisher.
Queries regarding rights and permissions should be addressed to: Orbis Books, P.O. Box 302, Maryknoll, NY 10545-0302.
Manufactured in the United States of America.
Manuscript editing and typesetting by Joan Weber Laflamme.
ISBN 978-1-62698-068-6

Library of Congress Cataloging-in-Publication Data

Names: Neafsey, John, author.
Title: Act justly, love tenderly : lifelong lessons in conscience and calling / John Neafsey.
Description: Maryknoll : Orbis Books, 2016. | Includes bibliographical references and index.
Identifiers: LCCN 2016009391 (print) | LCCN 2016021496 (ebook) | ISBN 9781626981928 (pbk. : alk. paper) | ISBN 9781608336647 (ebook)
Subjects: LCSH: Christian life. | Bible. Micah, VI, 8—Criticism, interpretation, etc.
Classification: LCC BV4501.3 .N39 2016 (print) | LCC BV4501.3 (ebook) | DDC
    248.4—dc23
LC record available at https://lccn.loc.gov/2016009391

*"With what gift shall I come into Yahweh's presence
and bow down before God on high?
Shall I come with holocausts,
with calves one year old?
Will he be pleased with rams by the thousand,
with libations of oil in torrents?
Must I give my first-born for what I have done wrong,
the fruit of my body for my own sin?"
What is good has been explained to you, man;
this is what Yahweh asks of you:
only this, to act justly, to love tenderly
and to walk humbly with your God.*

—MICAH 6:6–8, JERUSALEM BIBLE (1966)

CONTENTS

PREFACE

To do justice, to love kindness, to walk humbly with God—
these may embody all that we need to know in order to be
faithful and to be human.

—Walter Brueggemann

ACT JUSTLY, LOVE tenderly, walk humbly. The eighth verse of the sixth chapter of the book of the prophet Micah sums up so simply and beautifully how we are meant to live. Although Micah's words were originally addressed to the Jewish community in ancient Israel, I believe they are universally relevant, as applicable today as when they were first spoken almost three thousand years ago.

If Micah was right, each of us and all of us are called to embody our own share of justice, love, and humility during our short lives here on this earth. This, in a nutshell, is our fundamental human vocation. Each person is unique, and there are diverse ways of imagining the Caller in different cultures and traditions, but the call to be just and loving and humble applies to *everyone*: Christian, Muslim, Jew, Hindu, Buddhist, people of all the other diverse faith traditions of the world, and people of no particular faith tradition at all.

The process of writing this book has deepened my appreciation for the unique blend of deep spirituality and raw social conscience found in the writings of Micah and the other prophets of ancient Israel. My immersion in these texts has triggered considerable reflection on the psychology and spirituality of the prophetic vocation. It has also deepened my conviction that each of us is called to cultivate a kind of prophetic consciousness within the particular context of our own life and times.

This book is a sequel to my first book, *A Sacred Voice Is Calling: Personal Vocation and Social Conscience.*[1] Certain themes and ideas from that book will carry through this one, especially the link between personal calling and social conscience, and the conviction that vocation pertains to more than what we do for a living. Our calling is not only about what we do; it is about *who* we are and *how* we are. Vocation has to do with the *kind* of person we are called to become. The particular interest of this book is in how we respond to God's calling to become just and loving persons, at home and at work, for the sake of our communities, in an ever-expanding network of connection and solidarity with people both far and near.

In this book, for the sake of illustration, I explore the vocation stories of a number of exemplary people in the contemporary world whose lives have embodied a deep sense of justice, love, and humility. I also draw on experiences and stories from my professional life as a psychologist and from my family life as a husband and father. On a personal level, getting a little older and living through a number of important life experiences (moving through my fifties, parenting two children now in their tweens and teens, and caring for declining parents) have pushed me to think more concretely and seriously about callings in middle and later adulthood. *A Sacred Voice Is Calling* was particularly geared

---

[1] John Neafsey, *A Sacred Voice Is Calling: Personal Vocation and Social Conscience* (Maryknoll, NY: Orbis Books, 2006).

toward questions and issues relevant to vocational discernment for young adults. Crucial decisions about love and work that are made during our young adult years have a tremendous impact on the trajectory of the rest of our lives. But the sense of vocation is not only experienced in particular moments of decision in one phase of life. It is an unfolding process over the *whole* of life—from infancy through older adulthood, from the cradle to the grave. The Spirit speaks to us and calls us through each personal moment and experience in our lives. And so in this book I bring a lifespan perspective to bear on vocation as it is experienced in different ways over the course of our lives. I will not take an orderly developmental "phase" or "stage" approach but will simply try to be inclusive and expansive in considering how callings are experienced in response to different challenges and invitations at different times of life. For example, I explore the phenomenon of vocation in advanced age not from the perspective of the older adult, but from the vantage point of those who are called to care for declining elders.

My participation for the last several years in the *Seminar on Vocation across the Lifespan* at the Collegeville Institute for Ecumenical and Cultural Research has deepened my appreciation for the complexity and diversity of vocational experience over the course of life.[2] Kathleen Cahalan, the director of the Collegeville Institute Seminars, has been a gracious host and skilled facilitator for our twice-yearly meetings in the lovely setting of Saint John's University and Abbey in Collegeville, Minnesota. Other seminar participants include Laura Kelly Fanucci, Bonnie Miller-McLemore, Joyce Mercer, Jane Patterson, Matt Bloom, Katherine Turpin, and Jack Fortin. It has been a privilege to spend time

---

[2] For information about the Collegeville Institute Seminars' resources on vocation, which includes *Lives Explored*, a series of video narratives, as well as *Called to Life* and *Called to Work,* two small-group guides, and several books, see http://www.collegevilleinstitute.org/the-seminars/.

with such a thoughtful, conscientious, and faith-filled group of scholars for the purpose of exploring the high-stakes matter of what we are called to do with our lives. One of the fruits of the seminar is an edited volume of the writings of this fine group titled *Calling All Years Good: Vocation across the Lifespan.*[3]

I am grateful to Kathleen Cahalan for her thoughtful editing and for her consistent encouragement to find my own voice as a writer. I am also grateful to Robert Ellsberg for allowing me the opportunity to write again for Orbis Books, a press with a deep and longstanding commitment to social justice, reconciliation, and peace. It is an honor to work with him. I'm ever grateful to my wife, Maura, for her steadfast love, and also for her down-to-earth feedback and insight as I was writing this book. I'll never forget how she summed up the meaning of steadfast love in the story of the prophet Hosea: "God doesn't give up on us, even when we screw up." Finally, special thanks are due to my brother, Jim Neafsey, not only for his careful reading and help with improving the manuscript, but also for being an inspiring mentor and soul friend to me for as long as I can remember.

---

[3] Kathleen A. Cahalan and Bonnie J. Miller-McLemore, eds., *Calling All Years Good: Vocation across the Lifespan* (Grand Rapids, MI: Eerdmans, 2017). The Collegeville Institute Seminars also has produced a volume on interfaith perspectives on vocation (Kathleen A. Cahalan and Douglas J. Schuurman, eds., *Calling in Today's World: Voices from Eight Faith Perspectives* [Grand Rapids, MI: Eerdmans, 2016]).

INTRODUCTION

This is what Yahweh asks of you:
only this, to act justly,
to love tenderly
and to walk humbly with your God.
                              —Micah 6:8, Jerusalem Bible

THERE ARE A number of translations of Micah 6:8 in different versions of the Bible. All contain the same three essential elements: justice, love, and humility. The basic difference is in how the "love" part gets translated. My favorite, from which the title of this book comes, is from the Jerusalem Bible, which uses the phrase "to love *tenderly.*" The New Revised Standard Version uses "to love *kindness.*"

> And what does the Lord require of you,
> but to do justice,
> and to love kindness,
> and to walk humbly with your God?

I alternate between these translations throughout the book, exploring nuances of meaning in the different wordings along the way.

Micah was one of many prophets over a period of several centuries in ancient Israel. This intense, troubled, and often troublesome cast of characters includes those traditionally known as the major prophets (Isaiah, Jeremiah, Ezekiel, and Daniel) and the minor prophets (Micah, Hosea, Amos, Zechariah, Jonah, and others). The latter are considered minor not because their prophetic speech is any less inspired or ecstatic, but because their books are shorter.

The prophetic literature offers a rather wild and chaotic ride through visionary imagery; exquisite mystical poetry; arcane references to ancient peoples, places, and events; outpourings of divine mercy; and relentless denunciations of the religious and political authorities of the time. The writings of Walter Brueggemann, a popular and gifted biblical scholar who has an insightful way of linking ancient texts to contemporary issues of social concern, have been immensely helpful in appreciating not only the words spoken by the prophets, but also the kind of inner experiences that gave rise to them.[1]

The writings of Rabbi Abraham Joshua Heschel, especially his masterpiece *The Prophets*, have also been profoundly helpful. Heschel, a twentieth-century Jew, resonated in an almost uncanny way with the grief-stricken prophets of old, especially their acute sensitivity to evil and hypocrisy and their anguish over the suffering of the innocent.[2]

Some of the prophetic texts can be problematic and even off-putting. First, all of the prophetic books in the official canon of the Hebrew Bible (or Old Testament) were authored by men. At their inspired best, the oracles of these unusual men transcended

---

[1] See especially Walter Brueggemann, *The Prophetic Imagination* (Minneapolis, MN: Fortress Press, 2001).

[2] See Abraham Joshua Heschel, *The Prophets* (New York: Harper Perennial, 1962). Rabbi Heschel's personal story is told in "The Way of True Worship," in chap. 1.

and critiqued their culture. But there is plenty of evidence that the prophets were also culture-bound men of their times, whose language and metaphors sometimes reflect the values of the ancient patriarchal culture in which they lived.[3] Consequently, the prophetic literature is shot through with sexism, violence, vengeance, conquest, and questionable theological explanations and justifications for war and making war—all of which can potentially derail the progressive, contemporary reader. Timeless, transcendent, priceless gems are sprinkled liberally all through the prophetic books, but it is sometimes necessary to sift through all sorts of other material to find them. It is well worth the effort. I take an appreciative but critical approach.

Case in point: I once heard Daniel Berrigan, the Jesuit poet and war resister, do a memorable exegesis of an exquisite passage from Isaiah, the flow of which was spoiled by an unfortunate line containing a derogatory characterization of women.[4] When he reached this point in the text, Berrigan paused, rolled his eyes, and said, "I think we're going to have to forgive the prophet for this next line and move on!" The audience laughed.

This book is organized around Micah's triple summons to justice, love, and humility. I consider these not as three virtues or "three things to do," but rather, in the words of Brueggemann, as "three dimensions of a life of faithfulness, each of which depends

[3] For an excellent feminist analysis and critique of language and metaphors used by the prophets, see Julia M. O'Brien, *Challenging Prophetic Metaphors: Theology and Ideology in the Prophets* (Louisville, KY: Westminster John Knox, 2008).

[4] Daniel Berrigan, SJ, was perhaps most widely known for his participation in the Catonsville Nine, a group of Catholic antiwar activists who publicly burned draft records in protest against the Vietnam War at Catonsville, Maryland, in May 1968. For this action he served two years in federal prison. For insight into the thinking behind his role, see the letters between him and his brother Phil in *The Berrigan Letters: Personal Correspondence between Daniel and Philip Berrigan*, ed. Daniel Cosacchi and Eric Martin (Marknoll, NY: Orbis Books, 2016).

on and is reinforced by the other two."[5] Berrigan also notes the distinct but interdependent nature of the three dimensions in his meditations on Micah:

> And one wonders: Is the "command" triple or one? In any case, it would seem that the grand design of "doing justice" includes both tenderness and humility. And the command, issuing as it does from the heart of God, is also a clue and key—to the heart of God.[6]

The heart of God. There is a way that prophets of old like Micah—and modern-day prophets like Berrigan—seem to have unusual access to the heart of God, a kind of intimate personal knowledge of how God seems to be feeling about how things are going in this world at any given time. "The prophet hears God's voice," writes Heschel, "and feels His heart."[7] There is mysticism in this but no magic. Though it is tempting to see the prophets as extraordinary beings of a different order than the rest of us, they can also be regarded simply as unusually sensitive human beings who felt things very deeply—so deeply, it seems, that it is hard to tell where their own hearts leave off and the heart of God begins.

This is important, because there is a mysterious way that the stirrings of our own hearts can put us in touch with the heart of God. Stirrings of tender love, stirrings of conscience, stirrings of compassion in response to the pain and need of others, stirrings of indignation in response to unjust suffering—all these are con-

---

[5] See Walter Brueggemann, "Voices of the Night—Against Injustice," in *To Act Justly, Love Tenderly, Walk Humbly: An Agenda for Ministers*, ed. Walter Brueggemann, Sharon Parks, and Thomas Groome (New York: Paulist Press, 1986), 14–15.

[6] Daniel Berrigan, *Minor Prophets, Major Themes* (Marion, SD: Fortkamp Publishing/Rose Hill Books, 1995), 237.

[7] Heschel, *The Prophets*, 29.

stantly offering us clues and keys to the heart of God. Whether we are alert enough to pick up on the clues—and whether we have the courage to follow them—is another story. Callings often have their humble origins in such movements of the heart. Throughout this book I pay special attention to the affective and relational dimensions of callings to compassionate service and justice. I have a particular interest in the interrelationship of empathy and our sense of social conscience.

Gender, race, social class, religion, and culture can profoundly shape the ways that vocation is experienced by people from different backgrounds and in different situations. Sadly, this includes ways that callings can be stifled or needlessly frustrated by bias, lack of opportunity, and outright injustice. Much writing on vocation, including my own, has been done largely from the standpoint of privilege for the benefit of relatively privileged people (that is, mostly white, middle class, and college educated). The assumption is that financial and educational resources are in place, and that interesting options for fulfilling work are readily available from which to choose. The problem is that most people in the world are not in this privileged position and do not have the luxury of such discernment. Most have few or no options for meaningful work, and prevailing inequities limit their aspirations. Their primary concern is not authenticity but necessity and survival. In the interest of justice, such inequities are a major focus of this book.

1

ONLY THIS

"You are worried and distracted by many things; there is need of only one thing."

—Luke 10:41–42

IT IS EASY to forget what really matters during our short lives here on this earth. We get consumed by work pressures, family issues, money worries, health problems, emotional concerns—whatever happens to be the anxiety of the moment. Distracting voices in our culture and in ourselves make it hard to hear the still, small voice of the Spirit. Nonetheless, it is always there, whispering at the heart of things, trying to help us remember who we are, what we are here for, how we are called to live.

It would be hard to find a more succinct and beautiful prescription for how we are called to live than the eighth verse of the sixth chapter of the Book of Micah, in which the prophet reminds us that, in the end, all God really asks is that we "act justly, love tenderly, and walk humbly." *Only this.*

In this chapter I explore some of the ways this calling is experienced by diverse people in different contexts, beginning with some reflections on the prophets and what we know about the original context in which Micah's words were spoken. Our callings are necessarily experienced and lived out in the particulars of our historical and cultural and social circumstances, for better or for worse, in privilege or poverty, in ease or adversity. Regardless, all we have to work with is the raw material of who we are, in all our uniqueness and diversity and imperfection. Our vocation is also shaped and formed by the communities from which we come. We become persons through others.

THE WAY OF TRUE WORSHIP

Micah is best known for his lovely triple summons to justice, kindness, and humility, and for his prophecy that the Messiah would be born in Bethlehem (Mi 5:2). Little is known of his personal life. We do know that he lived in the eighth century BCE, roughly around the time of Isaiah and about one hundred years before Jeremiah. We know that he came from the rural farming area of Moresheth, which is a little south and west of Jerusalem, and that he apparently had quite a reputation as a prophet of doom. Almost a century later "Micah of Moresheth" is recalled in the Book of Jeremiah, which goes so far as to quote him:

> Zion shall be plowed as a field;
>   Jerusalem shall become a heap of ruins. (Jer
>   26:18)

Micah has been described by Walter Brueggemann as "the voice of the village peasant against the rapacious power of the state."[1] Much of the Book of Micah is taken up with the

---

[1] Walter Brueggemann, "Voices of the Night—Against Injustice," in *To Act Justly, Love Tenderly, Walk Humbly: An Agenda for Ministers*, ed. Walter Brueggemann, Sharon Parks, and Thomas Groome (Mahwah, NJ: Paulist Press, 1986), 7.

prophet's laments over how badly Israel has gone wrong, angry diatribes against deceitful shenanigans in high places, and threats of dire consequences.

> Alas for those who devise wickedness
> and evil deeds upon their beds!
> When the morning dawns, they perform it,
> because it is in their power.
> They covet fields, and seize them;
> houses, and take them away;
> they oppress householder and house,
> people and their inheritance.
> Therefore thus says the Lord:
> Now I am devising against this family an evil
> from which you cannot remove your necks;
> and you shall not walk haughtily,
> for it will be an evil time.
> On that day they will take up a taunt song
> against you. (Mi 2:1–4)

As a welcome break from the accusations and threats, Micah also offers some of the most beautiful imagery of healing and redemption to be found in all of scripture:

> They shall beat their swords into plowshares,
> and their spears into pruning hooks;
> nation shall not lift sword against nation,
> neither shall they learn war any more. (Mi
> 4:3; see Is 2:4)

For the most part, though, Micah is not "nice." He has a definite edge. He is admired for this by Daniel Berrigan, who is also known for his prophetic edginess. "Micah, God help us, is judgmental," says Berrigan, with a touch of sarcasm for those who shy away from prophetic criticizing. "He stands before great or lowly, as a surrogate judge, ferocious, incandescent with indignation and fury. . . . No other prophet equals Micah in the furious denunciation loosed upon chiefs of temple and state."[2]

The prophets were of more than scholarly interest to Abraham Joshua Heschel, who himself possessed a prophetic consciousness that was manifested again and again in his own life and times as a twentieth-century Jew. Polish-born Heschel lost most of his family in the Holocaust. As a descendant of a distinguished line of Hasidic rabbis, Heschel came by his prophetic conscious-ness honestly. In 1938, after completing his doctoral studies in Berlin, he was arrested by the Gestapo and deported back to his homeland. It happened that Heschel had arranged to leave Poland to take a teaching position in the United States just a few weeks before the Nazi invasion in 1939. Sadly, his sister Esther was killed during the invasion; his mother and a second sister, Gittel, were murdered by the Nazis; and a third sister, Devorah, died at Auschwitz.[3]

As an American citizen in the decades following the Ho-locaust, and as a citizen of the world, Heschel could not help becoming deeply engaged in the great moral issues of his time: the civil rights movement and efforts to end the Vietnam War. As a person who knew persecution, he was horrified by racism in American society. In the 1960s he formed an extraordinary personal friendship with Dr. Martin Luther King, Jr. Significantly, each described the other as a prophet. In 1965, Heschel walked alongside King in the historic march from Selma to Montgom-ery. (He is seen in iconic photos of the event with his long white beard, as if he had just time-traveled to twentieth-century Alabama

---

[2] Daniel Berrigan, *Minor Prophets, Major Themes* (Marion, SD: Fortkamp Publishing/Rose Hill Books, 1995), 215, 220.

[3] For an excellent short biography of Abraham Joshua Heschel, see his daughter Susannah Heschel's introduction to *Abraham Joshua Heschel: Essential Writings* (Maryknoll, NY: Orbis Books, 2011).

from the eighth century BCE.) Remembering the Selma experience, Heschel writes: "I felt a sense of the Holy in what I was doing. . . . Even without words, our march was worship. I felt my legs were praying."[4]

Ten days before his assassination on April 4, 1968, Dr. King spoke at a birthday celebration to honor Rabbi Heschel:

> "Here and there, we find those who refuse to remain silent behind the safe security of stained-glass windows, and they are forever seeking to make the great ethical insights of our Judeo-Christian heritage relevant in this day and in this age. I feel that Rabbi Heschel is one of the persons who is relevant at all times, always standing with prophetic insights to guide us through these difficult days."[5]

Heschel was also haunted by the sinfulness and criminality of the Vietnam War. "To speak about God and remain silent on Vietnam," he said, "is blasphemous."[6] His daughter Susannah remembers her father's inner turmoil and sleepless nights over the war; she also recalls a striking explanation he once gave for his participation in public protests against the war:

> A journalist once asked my father why he had come to a demonstration against the war in Vietnam. "I am here because I cannot pray," my father told him. Confused and a bit annoyed, the journalist asked him, "What do you mean you can't pray so you come to a demonstration against

---

[4] Heschel is quoted in Edward K. Kaplan, *Spiritual Radical: Abraham Joshua Heschel in America: 1940–1972* (New Haven, CT: Yale University Press, 2007), 225.

[5] *Abraham Joshua Heschel,* 38.

[6] Abraham Joshua Heschel, "The Moral Outrage of Vietnam," in *Vietnam: Crisis of Conscience*, ed. R. M. Brown, A. J. Heschel, and R. Novak (New York: Herder and Herder, 1967), 49.

the war?" And my father replied, "Whenever I open the prayerbook, I see before me images of children burning from napalm."[7]

As someone who "prayed with his feet" for African Americans, and who *couldn't* pray because he was so upset about the suffering of Vietnamese children, Heschel had much in common with prophets like Isaiah and Amos and Micah, who were appalled by the kind of numbing religiosity that functions as a conscience-soothing distraction from social injustice and a world of hurt.

> I hate, I despise your festivals,
>> and I take no delight in your solemn as-
>>> semblies. . . .
> Take away from me the noise of your songs;
>> I will not listen to the melody of your harps.
> But let justice roll down like waters,
>> And righteousness like an ever-flowing
>>> stream. (Am 5:21, 23–24)

According to Heschel, Micah poses the most urgent question of religious existence: "What is the way of true worship?"[8] The prophet's answer is simple but profound:

> only this, to act justly,
> to love tenderly
> and to walk humbly with your God.

This inspiring summons to justice, kindness, and humility is easier to put into noble-sounding words than it is actually to *live* in real life. And the devil—or, rather, the Spirit—is definitely in

---

[7] *Abraham Joshua Heschel,* 17.

[8] Abraham Joshua Heschel, *The Prophets* (New York: Harper Perennial, 1962), 129.

the details of whether and how it is taken to heart in the lives of real persons and communities. It all depends.

FROM OUR MOTHER'S WOMB

Acknowledged or not, the sense of personal vocation potentially begins very early and unfolds over the entire lifespan of the human person. Looking back over our lives, it is sometimes possible to detect early inklings of vocation in certain childhood memories and experiences. Though we may not be fully conscious of their meaning and significance at the time we are going through them, we may later recognize the origins and evolution of our callings through a reflective process of "retrospective sensemaking" or "reading life backward."[9]

Sometimes other people are able to sense special talents or vocational potentials in us even when we are quite young. Along these lines there is a lovely story from the life of Black Elk, the great Lakota Sioux visionary and healer. At the age of nine, young Black Elk became severely ill, tenuously hovering between life and death in a coma-like state of unconsciousness for twelve days.[10] When the little boy finally began to recover, an intuitive older shaman by the name of Whirlwind Chaser observed to Black Elk's parents: "Your boy is sitting there in a sacred manner. I do not know what it is, but there is something special for him to do."[11] Interestingly, in many indigenous cultures childhood

---

[9] *Retrospective sensemaking* is a phrase that comes from the work of Matt Bloom, a member of the *Seminar on Vocation across the Lifespan*. He directs the *Wellbeing at Work* research project at the University of Notre Dame. The phrase captures the process by which people recognize, through life review and reflection, the origin and development of callings over the course of their lives. *Reading life backward* is a phrase used by James Hillman in *The Soul's Code: In Search of Character and Calling* (New York: Random House, 1996), 7.

[10] See John G. Neihardt, *Black Elk Speaks: Being the Life Story of a Holy Man of the Oglala Sioux* (Lincoln: University of Nebraska Press, 1932), 20–47.

[11] Ibid., 49.

illness is not always interpreted only as an unfortunate intrusion; it may be seen as a painful but necessary experience that potentially prepares the young person to serve the community as a healer, following the archetypal vocational pattern of the *wounded healer*. Similarly, many modern people also mark the beginning of their inclinations toward the helping and healing professions in personal experiences of suffering earlier in their lives.[12]

Some gifted personalities with a mystical or prophetic bent look back on their lives with a recognition that a sacred purpose or destiny was there for them all along, perhaps even from the very beginning. We see this very distinctly in the vocation stories of prophets like Isaiah and Jeremiah:

> The Lord called me before I was born,
>> while I was in my mother's womb he named
>> me. (Is 49:1)

> Now the word of the Lord came to me saying,
>> "Before I formed you in the womb I knew
>> you,
>> and before you were born I consecrated you;
>> I appointed you a prophet to the nations."
>> (Jer 1:4–5)

It is unlikely, of course, that Isaiah and Jeremiah had actual memories of being called to their prophetic vocations before they were born. But there is no doubt they possessed a deep sense of personal mission or destiny, so much so that they were convinced it was the very reason for which they were born. The later recognition by the prophet of this lifelong sense of calling

---

[12] See John Neafsey, *A Sacred Voice Is Calling: Personal Vocation and Social Conscience* (Maryknoll, NY: Orbis Books, 2006), 109–30.

is seen by Brueggemann as a "reflective authorization after the fact":

> I use the term "call" not in the sense of a datable experience, but as a sense that one's own life has a theonomous cast, is deeply referred to the purposes of God, which gives freedom and distance and perspective in relation to all other concerns. Such a call is not an event, but an ongoing dynamic of a growing and powerful claim. One's embrace of a call may mature in time and grow beyond the innocence of the outset.[13]

The sense of personal vocation, at least in the "innocence of the outset," can be likened to a seed of sacred potential in the soul of each human person. The full, mature expression of this potential may be "not yet," but our spiritual essence is already there from the very beginning. James Hillman refers to this as the *acorn theory,* which holds that "each person bears a uniqueness that asks to be lived and that is already present before it can be lived."[14] This applies not only to infancy and childhood, but to *every* phase of our life's journey; throughout our journey we are always, at any given time, both "already" and "not yet." The "not yet" always remains as a mysterious, hidden potential waiting to be expressed, evoked, called forth. But the "already" is who we actually are, right now, in all our imperfection, wherever we happen to be in our process of development and growth.[15] The

---

[13] Walter Brueggemann, *The Hopeful Imagination: Prophetic Voices in Exile* (Philadelphia: Fortress Press, 1986), 18.

[14] Hillman, *The Soul's Code,* 6.

[15] See Joyce Mercer, "Toward a Feminist Practical Theology of Childhood," in *Welcoming Children: A Practical Theology of Childhood* (Atlanta: Chalice, 2005). Also see Joyce Mercer and Dori Grinenko Baker, *Lives to Offer: Accompanying Youth on Their Vocational Quests* (Cleveland: Pilgrim Press, 2007).

words of a widely known gospel song are consoling to all of us
who are still works in progress: "Please be patient with me, God
is not through with me yet."[16]

The "uniqueness that asks to be lived" is another way of
expressing the notion of the *true self*. The *uniqueness* is our true
name, and the *asking* is the call to live the truth of who we are,
to fulfill the purpose for which we were born. This is one way
to understand what Isaiah may have meant by saying he was
"named" before he was born. Thomas Merton wrote of this idea
that each human person has an essential inner self calling from
within for realization or actualization:

> In Sufism, Zen Buddhism and in many other religious or
> spiritual traditions, emphasis is placed on the call to fulfill
> certain obscure yet urgent potentialities in the ground of
> one's being, to "become someone" that one already (po-
> tentially) is, the person one is truly meant to be. Zen calls
> this awakening a recognition of "your original face before
> you were born."[17]

Merton is referring to a famous Zen koan (a statement or
question meant to provoke enlightenment) associated with Hui
Neng, a Chinese Zen master who lived in the latter part of the
seventh century:

> Show me your original face,
> the face you had before your parents were
> born."[18]

---

[16] Sim Wilson, Jr., "Please Be Patient with Me," © Peermusic III, Ltd., 1979.

[17] See Thomas Merton, "Final Integration: Toward a 'Monastic Therapy,'" in
Contemplation in a World of Action (Notre Dame, IN: University of Notre Dame
Press, 1998 <1971>), 201–2.

[18] Beatrice Bruteau, *What We Can Learn from the East* (New York: Crossroad,
1995), 115.

Before our *parents* were born goes back even farther than our mother's womb, suggesting that our true identity ultimately belongs to a dimension beyond the bounds of our finite, personal lifetime.

William Johnston, an Irish Jesuit who spent the greater part of his life immersed in the dialogue between Zen Buddhism and Christianity, likened the original face in Zen to "one's true self as it existed in the mind of God for all eternity." He notes, however, that a distinguishing feature of the Judeo-Christian tradition is that the self is not only unique, but is "uniquely loved and chosen."[19]

Although matters of authenticity and the true self can sound esoteric, one does not have to be a mystic or Zen master to appreciate what it feels like to be "the real me." Ordinary people have experiences all the time that put us in touch with our authentic selves. This can be as simple as acknowledging our true feelings about something important, becoming aware of our genuine desires and inclinations, or recognizing that we feel more alive when we are engaged in certain activities that are in tune with our natural bent. In such moments we feel a sense of authenticity, a connection to something within that feels real.

The link with vocation is that we are called, first of all, to be *ourselves*. Gerard Manley Hopkins has a beautiful way of putting this in his poem "As Kingfishers Catch Fire":

> Each mortal thing does one thing and the same:
> Deals out that being indoors each one dwells;
> Selves—goes itself; *myself* it speaks and spells,
> Crying *What I do is me: for that I came.*[20]

---

[19] William Johnston, *The Mirror Mind: Spirituality and Transformation* (San Francisco: Harper and Row, 1981), 38.

[20] "As Kingfishers Catch Fire," in *Gerard Manley Hopkins: The Major Works* (Oxford: Oxford University Press, 1986), 129.

In certain moments and experiences we hear echoes or reverberations of our own inner truth—of that being inside. Rumi, a Sufi poet from the thirteenth century, wrote poignantly of this in "The Reed Flute's Song." In the poem a flute notices its natural mournful sound and remembers where it came from:

> "Since I was cut from the reedbed,
> I have made this crying sound."[21]

The flute seems to realize that it sounds the way it does because of the kind of wood from which it was cut. Similarly, each of us has experiences that put us in touch with the truth of our own nature, what we are made of, what we are made *for*. Recognizing "what sounds like me" or "what feels like me" are the key tasks in such discernment. The greater part of my psychotherapeutic work involves helping people to notice such things in their lives. But conscious awareness is not enough; the crucial next step is to take responsibility for such insights by finding the courage to live in ways that honor the self-discovery. Easier said than done, but better to be ourselves than to waste time trying to be someone we're *not*.

The mournfulness of the flute is also perhaps connected with being separated from its original home among the other reeds. There is a sense of loneliness and grief inherent in the process of vocational self-discovery, which often requires a certain psychological separation and differentiation from our community and family of origin.[22]

---

[21] Jelaluddin Rumi, "The Reed Flute's Song," in *The Essential Rumi*, exp. ed., translated by Coleman Barks (New York: HarperOne, 2004), 17–19.

[22] Jung's term for the process of becoming an authentic individual is *individuation*. For his exploration of the link between individuation and vocation, see Carl G. Jung, "The Development of Personality," in *The Development of Personality* (New York: Bollingen Foundation, 1954).

In a period of inner turmoil during my young adult years I had a memorable dream that contained striking images relevant to these matters of authenticity and destiny. At the time I was struggling with the dilemma of whether to "play it safe" in certain life choices or take the more risky individual path of following my own interests and instincts. This was the dream:

> *I am aware that I am going on a journey and that I have a choice between two destinations. The first option (which feels rather boring) is to accompany my parents on a family vacation to a touristy high-rise hotel on the beach in Hawaii. The other option (which feels both scary and exciting) is to go on a pilgrimage to Jerusalem. I know deep down that Jerusalem is where I really want to go, but there is a sense of trepidation because I know that I will have to make the journey to Jerusalem on my own. Nonetheless, as the dream concludes, I feel a sense of inner resolve to set out on the pilgrimage. "I would rather be alone and lonely in Jerusalem," I say to myself, "than anyplace else on earth."*

The dream did not provide advice or direction about the choices I was considering at the time. But it offered a stirring image of life as a pilgrimage to a sacred destination—as opposed to a superficial tourist trip on the surface of life—along with encouragement to not let fear or convention hold me back.[23]

The image of a geographic pilgrimage was, I think, symbolic of an inner journey to authentic selfhood that would require the courage to differentiate from family and go my own way. A certain aloneness or loneliness is an inevitable consequence of

---

[23] The image of Jerusalem is rich and complex. See, for example, Thomas Merton, "From Pilgrimage to Crusade," in *Mystics and Zen Masters* (New York: Dell Publishing, 1961). See also my reflections on the Church of the Holy Sepulchre in *Crucified People: The Suffering of the Tortured in Today's World* (Maryknoll, NY: Orbis Books, 2014).

making choices based on our authentic desires and dreams rather than just going along with what others are doing—or with what others think we *should* be doing. For me, there was also a mysterious sense of consolation that I would ultimately *not* be all alone, because *God* would be with me every step of the way. I was not called only to do my own thing; I was uniquely loved and chosen.

THE NATURAL FACTS

Each human person has a unique spiritual essence or identity, but we are also *embodied* creatures, born into this particular body and these particular circumstances.

In *The Soul's Code: In Search of Character and Calling,* James Hillman offers a sharp critique of the soullessness of much contemporary psychological thinking, especially the idea that the development of human personality is a predictable outcome of the interplay between genetics and environment. This paradigm, he says, "omits something essential—the particularity you feel to be you."[24] Although nature and nurture cannot fully account for the mystery of the human person, they are certainly foundational and formative dimensions of our personal existence. Our genetic makeup determines fundamental components of our bodily identity, including, among other things, our gender, the color of our skin, our body type, and our sexual orientation.

If we are called, first of all, to be *ourselves*, then we must work with the raw material that we have been given. We do not choose whether we are black or white, male or female, gay or straight; these are *givens*.[25] They are the natural, God-given facts

---

[24] Hillman, *The Soul's Code,* 6.

[25] Gender can be distinguished from gender identity, which has to do with a person's internal, personal sense of being a man or a woman. For transgender persons this differs from the sex they were assigned at birth.

of who we are. And, if each of us is loved and chosen, then we are loved and chosen *as we are*.[26]

How we *feel* about ourselves, of course, is another story, as is the matter of whether things like race, gender, and sexual orientation work to our advantage or disadvantage in the world in which we live. Sadly, the effects of bias and discrimination can complicate and undermine the process of vocational self-discovery for persons who happen to be the "wrong" skin color, gender, sexual orientation, body type, or any other category of difference that makes a person less desirable according to prevailing cultural prejudices. When people are unsure if they are accepted, respected, safe, and worthy of equal treatment, they are more vulnerable to the toxic and undermining influences of self-doubt, self-hatred, insecurity, and shame.

The vocational casualties of injustice and prejudice are wasted human potential and frustrated callings. Dreams are sometimes deferred due to lack of opportunity and outright injustice. Authenticity needs must be put aside for the sake of necessity and survival. Young people are often tempted to give up, drop out, check out, or act out. Opportunities for joy and fulfillment are missed, and the community is deprived of gifts and contributions that could have made a difference for the better.

Historical inequities and prevailing societal prejudices may determine what part of town (or what part of the world) we are born into, the quality of the schools we attend (or whether we get to attend school at all), the attitudes of authorities toward our community, the degree of danger we face in our surroundings,

---

[26] Kathleen A. Cahalan has done some interesting work on the "grammar of vocation" in developing a contemporary theology of vocation. The preposition *as* (as in "called *as* we are") is one of eight prepositions that can be used to describe the sense of vocation in more dynamic and relational ways: *by, to, as, from, for, through, in,* and *within.* See Kathleen A. Cahalan, *Call It What It Is* (Grand Rapids, MI: Eerdmans, 2016).

whether we have access to decent food and health care and housing, and the degree to which we have to contend with officially or
unofficially unacknowledged limits on our vocational aspirations.

James Baldwin, one of the great literary voices of the twen-
tieth century, happened to be black and gay in times and places
that were particularly unfriendly to persons who were either of
these things. In a 1962 letter to his fourteen-year-old nephew,
who was then growing up in New York City's Harlem, Baldwin
offered some prophetic perspective on racism and the hazards
it presents to the developing hearts and minds of young people:

> You were born where you were born and faced the future
> that you faced because you were black and for no other
> reason. The limits of your ambition were thus expected to
> be settled. You were born into a society which spelled out
> with brutal clarity and in as many ways as possible that you
> were a worthless human being. You were not expected to
> aspire to excellence. You were expected to make peace with
> mediocrity. . . . The details and symbols of your life have
> been deliberately constructed to make you believe what
> white people say about you. Please try to remember that
> what they believe, as well as what they do and cause you
> to endure, does not testify to your inferiority but to their
> inhumanity and fear.[27]

Holding on to one's personal dignity and aspirations to authenticity and excellence may require extraordinary inner effort
and communal support in order to counter or contain the dis-
couraging and corrosive effects of racism. Some people may have

---

[27] For this version of James Baldwin's letter, see "A Letter to My Nephew,"
The Progressive (December 1962). The letter was later adapted and published
as an essay titled "My Dungeon Shook: Letter to My Nephew on the One
Hundredth Anniversary of the Emancipation," in James Baldwin, *The Fire Next
Time* (New York: The Dial Press, 1963), 1–10.

to work "twice as hard" and be "twice as good" with no guarantees that they still won't have to settle for "half as much."Ta-Nehisi Coates, a contemporary African American writer who is regarded as one of Baldwin's literary successors, refers to this exhausting and painful state of affairs as "the great American injury."[28]

My children have helped to raise my consciousness about issues of race and gender. Bryan, now a teenager, was born in Guatemala. He is of Mayan descent, and his skin is a beautiful shade of brown. He likes to wear hoodies. Since the killing of young Trayvon Martin (an African American teen wearing a hoodie at the time of his death) in February 2012, I have often thought about my son's vulnerability to prejudice and stereotypes as a young man of color. For example, when we were in a store recently, I found myself coaching him about how it would be advisable to keep his hood down and his hands out of his pockets, so as not to draw suspicion from anyone who might have issues with male teenagers of color. This prompted a painful but necessary discussion of skin color and the need for a certain realistic awareness and vigilance about such matters in public situations. The high stakes involved moved me to tears when I saw a striking contemporary painting of the pieta in which both the Madonna and Jesus are rendered as African American. Inspired by the Trayvon Martin incident, the figure of Jesus is wearing a hoodie and clutching a bag of Skittles in his lifeless hand.[29]

My daughter, Rosie, also comes from Guatemala. When she was in fifth grade, she was assigned to memorize and recite a

---

[28] Ta-Nehisi Coates, *Between the World and Me* (New York: Spiegel & Grau, 2015), 142.

[29] Margo Humphrey's painting "Fear Not: I Got You" (2013, lithograph with gold leaf, courtesy of Anchor Graphics and the Arts Program of the University of Maryland University College) was used for the cover of a recent book by Kelly Brown Douglas, *Stand Your Ground: Black Bodies and the Justice of God* (Maryknoll, NY: Orbis Books, 2015).

poem in front of her class. We settled on "Harlem" by Langston Hughes:

> What happens to a dream deferred?
>
>> Does it dry up
>> like a raisin in the sun?
>> Or fester like a sore—
>> and then run?
>> Does it stink like rotten meat?
>> Or crust and sugar over—
>> like a syrupy sweet?
>> Maybe it just sags
>> like a heavy load.
>
> *Or does it explode?*[30]

As Rosie practiced reciting the poem, we talked about some of its possible meanings. This happened to be April 2015, just as the city of Baltimore was erupting into violent riots triggered by the death of an African American man named Freddie Grey, who had suffered a spinal injury in police custody. It was not hard to make the connection between the rageful explosion in inner-city Baltimore and the bitter disappointment of deferred dreams in the poem.

Frustrated callings and deferred dreams resulting from gender discrimination are also a common feature of women's lives in both church and society. A few years ago our family was invited by a friend to attend the ritual of her ordination to the priesthood. Because we are Roman Catholics, it is not part of our experience to see a woman presiding at the altar; I thought it might

---

[30] Langston Hughes, "Harlem," (1951), in *Selected Poems of Langston Hughes* (New York: Random House, 1990).

be good for Rosie to experience something different. When she realized that the person to be ordained was a woman, she exclaimed, "But, Daddy, women can't be priests!" This prompted an honest, consciousness-raising discussion for all of us about how church and society sometimes put ceilings in place that set artificial limits on the dreams and aspirations of women.

UNCHOSEN CIRCUMSTANCES AND THE BLUES

Just as we do not choose the body we are born with, we do not have a choice about the circumstances into which we are born. For better or for worse, we were born into *this* particular family with its own unique history and character, *this* social location in the hierarchy of society, *this* ethnic or religious group, *this* particular place and time out of all possible times and places in history. Where we start does not necessarily determine where we end up, but our roots certainly have profound formative influences on the development of our identity and character.

I don't believe it is possible to discern the hand of God in why some are born into poverty and others into privilege, or why some are blessed with resources and options while others seem cursed with little or nothing. For the privileged, humility is the only fitting response to the suffering and misfortune of others. I agree with liberation theologians like Gustavo Gutiérrez and Jon Sobrino, who are clear that poverty and injustice are *not* the will of God but are rather the historical and structural outcomes of human evil and injustice.

Not so long ago I came to know a young asylum seeker from East Africa. He is a kind, decent, devout Sufi Muslim with a deep sense of conscience and integrity. He happened to have been born into desperate poverty, and his minority tribal group has often been the target of murderous ethnic violence. He lost a beloved parent and several siblings in the bloody mayhem and anarchy that have plagued his homeland. I was deeply moved by his story and humbled by his courage and resilience and perseverance against all odds. In gratitude for my modest efforts to help, he once told me that he prayed for me every day. I was grateful for this, because I am sure the prayers of people like him go straight to the heart of God, who is known in his tradition as the Most Merciful.

Regardless of circumstances, everyone has a capacity to sense a calling. Callings come to people as they are, wherever they are, in whatever circumstances they find themselves. Because a person has limited options does not mean he or she does not have a calling; it just means the shape or character of the calling will necessarily be different. It all depends. For some, the calling may be to escape the constricting confines of their background through a kind of upward mobility out of poverty, perhaps by being the first person in their family to get an education, or perhaps through migration to another country in search of a better situation. For others, the call may be to stay put, maybe to fight for change of unjust social conditions in the context of their own communities. For many, the most challenging call is to try, humbly and patiently, to preserve a sense of personal dignity in undignified circumstances.

There is a saying of Saint Irenaeus: "The glory of God is the human being fully alive." Archbishop Oscar Romero of El Salvador, who was slain by a government assassin in 1980, adapted the saying just a little to the context of unjust poverty and violence in his homeland: "The glory of God is the *poor person* fully alive."[31] In the absence of substantial social change of structures that *make* people poor and *keep* people poor, we might imagine the poor person fully alive as someone who is not only able to

---

[31] Oscar Romero, address at the University of Louvain, February 2, 1980: "The Political Dimension of the Faith from the Perspective of the Option for the Poor," in *Voice of the Voiceless: Four Pastoral Letters and Other Statements* (Maryknoll, NY: Orbis Books, 1985), 187.

keep his or her body alive but who is able to hold on to a sense of personal dignity and joy *in spite of* oppressive circumstances.

In some circumstances our interior spiritual attitude may be the only thing we *can* change. According to Victor Frankl, whether suffering becomes an occasion for spiritual triumph or defeat depends entirely on our capacity to discover a meaning or purpose in it. Frankl, an Austrian psychiatrist who wrote of his personal experiences of extreme suffering in the Nazi concentration camps in the classic *Man's Search for Meaning*, emphasizes the capacity to *choose* our attitude toward suffering regardless of external circumstances.

> Everything can be taken away but one thing, the last of human freedoms—to choose one's attitude in any given set of circumstances. . . . Fundamentally, even in the worst of circumstances, we can decide what shall become of ourselves mentally and spiritually, retaining our human dignity even in a concentration camp.[32]

Frankl's analysis applies not only to the extreme cruelty of the concentration camp experience, but to any oppressive or demoralizing situation that cannot easily be escaped or changed or controlled.

There is an analogous idea in the writings of Ralph Ellison on the African American experience. Ellison explores the meaning and function of the musical form of the blues. In an exquisite passage from his classic essay "Richard Wright's Blues," Ellison writes of the capacity not only to *endure* but also to *transcend* suffering through a particular quality of consciousness that is characteristic of the blues:

---

[32] Victor Frankl, *Man's Search for Meaning* (New York: Washington Square Press, 1984 <1946>), 86. Some of the material in this section is adapted from John Neafsey, *A Sacred Voice Is Calling*.

The blues is an impulse to keep the painful details and episodes of a brutal experience alive in one's aching consciousness, to finger its jagged grain, and to transcend it, not by the consolation of philosophy but by squeezing from it a near-tragic, near-comic lyricism. As a form, the blues is an autobiographical chronicle of personal catastrophe expressed lyrically.[33]

Ellison is talking about something very deep: the capacity for personal triumph over adversity, not by denying the pain, but by consciously experiencing and expressing it in such a way that it is transformed into something beautiful. Just listen to Robert Johnson, one of the great early masters of the blues from the Mississippi Delta:

> Well, the blues, is a achin' old heart disease
> The blues, is a low-down achin' heart disease
> Like consumption, killin' me by degrees.
>
> I got stones in my passway, and my road seem
>   dark as night
> I got stones in my passway, and my road seem
>   dark as night
> I have pains in my heart, they have taken my
>   appetite.[34]

---

[33] Ralph Ellison, "Richard Wright's Blues," in *Shadow and Act* (New York: Random House, 1995 <1965>), 77–78.

[34] Robert Johnson (1911–38) was one of the great bluesmen of the Mississippi Delta. The stark emotional intensity, urgency, and expressiveness of his singing and guitar playing are legendary. He died tragically when he was only twenty-seven years old. His unforgettable music is available on *Robert Johnson: The Complete Recordings* (Sony, 1990). For an excellent biography, see Peter Guralnick, *Searching for Robert Johnson* (New York: Plume, 1998). The two extracts here are from "Preaching Blues" and "Stones in My Passway."

Although the blues came out of the uniquely cruel and oppressive experience of African Americans, there are parallels in the lives of people from all walks of life. In my work as a psychologist I am privileged to witness the courage of men and women as they wrestle with their own pain.[35] Sometimes their pain has resulted from their own choices, but often it is related to unchosen circumstances: old hurts and resentments and disappointments, emotional baggage from repressive religious upbringings, illness, loss, trauma of various kinds—the list of personal catastrophes goes on and on.

The aim of the "talking cure" is not just to get over the pain but to discern its meanings in the hope of discovering a healing and redemptive way forward. Healing always seems to occur, first of all, in the inner relationship of a person to himself or herself. Using the language of Micah, they learn to treat *themselves* more justly, to love *themselves* more tenderly. This makes it possible to move from feeling defeated and humiliated by life to a kinder, more dignified sense of acceptance and humility about all the things that cannot be controlled.

WE BECOME PERSONS THROUGH OTHERS

There is a certain loneliness inherent in the process of vocational self-discovery. If we are to be authentic persons, no one else can think our thoughts, feel our feelings, or make our choices for us. Each of us is ultimately responsible for our own decisions in high-stakes matters of conscience and the heart. The paradox is that *none* of us can do this alone. We need others to help us discover who we are, what we are good at, how we may be able to help.

Earlier in this chapter I recounted an important dream in which I realized it would be necessary for me to set out alone

---

[35] Neil Altman offers thoughtful reflections on all these issues in *The Analyst in the Inner City: Race, Class, and Culture through a Psychoanalytic Lens* (New York: Routledge, 2010).

on a pilgrimage to Jerusalem. On the surface, the symbolism of the dream seemed to portray vocation as a solitary journey. On a deeper level, though, all my associations to the dream in the context of my life at the time were suggestive of a call to deepening relationship and connection with others. First, there was a growing hunger for connection with God, who was not only the destination (symbolized by the holy city), but who would accompany me as a kind of unseen companion all along the way. Also, though I had thought for some time about becoming a priest, at the time of the dream it was becoming increasingly clear to me that my own calling was not to the single, celibate life of the priest, but rather to the day-to-day intimacy and companionship of marriage and family. I was also coming to the realization that I was not suited to work within the context of the institutional church but was more drawn to a secular ministry of helping and healing souls in the world through work as a psychologist.

Perhaps most crucial was my relationship with an important mentor throughout this process of vocational self-discovery. For a period of about four years during my mid-twenties I was blessed to be able to work with Fred Maples, an analyst trained in the school of Jungian depth psychology and dreamwork. Fred also happened to be a Jesuit priest who was well-versed in the traditions of Ignatian spirituality and discernment. He listened carefully and deeply to me each week, making it possible for me safely to feel and explore important aspects of my emerging identity. He became for me what was known in early Irish Christianity as an *anam cara* (soul friend). Each week, after I talked about how things were going on the surface of my life, I distinctly remember how Fred would encourage me to explore what was happening on a deeper level by inviting me to share a dream: "Well, now let's hear what your *unconscious* has to say." In this way, through the experience of being heard and understood, I learned to listen more deeply to *myself*.

D. W. Winnicott, a wise and compassionate British psycho-analyst and pediatrician, coined the term *holding environment* to describe a certain quality of relationship that facilitates the process of self-discovery and personal growth.[36] Winnicott was particularly interested in parallels between psychotherapy and the nurturing mother–child relationship. He thought and wrote a lot about the quality of the empathic attunement of the parent or caregiver to the needs and feelings of the child, especially its impact on the child's developing sense of self and the capacity to feel *real* by knowing his or her true feelings. He highlighted the importance of the parent's capacity to serve as a *mirror* by notic-ing and reflecting back to the child what the child is feeling or experiencing at any given time: "You look excited." "You seem a little sad." "You look upset." "It seems as though you really enjoy doing that." Through being *seen* and *felt* the child begins to see and feel himself or herself more clearly.

Good, or at least *good enough*, mothering or fathering is an early model for a diverse variety of other nurturing relation-ships that can develop beyond the family at any time over the course of our lives. These might include a connection with a respected mentor in the world of school or work, a psychothera-pist, a spiritual director, a trusted colleague or peer, a sibling, a spouse or partner, a friend who becomes a soul friend—really, *anyone* who becomes emotionally significant enough to us to have a formative influence on our development as a person. Significant others like these have been referred to as "those who count."[37] Like good parents, they provide essential mirroring that helps us learn to recognize our authentic selves. James Fowler

---

[36] See, for example, "The Theory of the Parent-Infant Relationship," in D. W. Winnicott, *The Maturational Processes and the Facilitating Environment: Stud-ies in the Theory of Emotional Development* (New York: International Universities Press, 1966), 37–55.

[37] See Sharon Parks, "Love Tenderly," in Brueggemann, Parks, and Groome, *To Act Justly, Love Tenderly, Walk Humbly*, 33.

summarized the process like this:"I see you seeing me; I see the you I think you see."[38]

It is crucial to notice and appreciate the presence of potential mentors and soul friends in our lives and to make good use of them while we have the chance. In their absence we must use our best instincts to search for the kind of person who can fill the bill. In *The Book of Questions,* the great Chilean poet Pablo Neruda asks a key question:"Whom can I ask what I came to make happen in this world?"[39]

Communities also have an important mentoring influence in our lives. In *Big Questions, Worthy Dreams,* Sharon Daloz Parks expands the traditional two-person model of the mentoring relationship to include the nurturing influence of *mentoring communities* in various contexts. These might include churches, schools, retreat centers, and any other kinds of intentional community that offer a hospitable, supportive space where people can gather to consider deeper questions about the meaning, purpose, and direction of their lives.[40]

---

[38] James W. Fowler, *Stages of Faith: The Psychology of Human Development and the Quest for Meaning* (San Francisco: HarperCollins, 1995), 46. I'm indebted to Joyce Mercer (a member of the *Vocation Across the Lifespan Seminar*) and Dori Grinenko Baker for their insightful exploration of mentoring and mirroring in the lives of adolescents in their excellent book *Lives to Offer: Accompanying Youth on Their Vocational Quests* (Cleveland: Pilgrim Press, 2007).

[39] Pablo Neruda, *The Book of Questions* (Port Townsend, WA: Copper Canyon Press, 2001 <1974>), 31.

[40] Sharon Daloz Parks, *Big Questions, Worthy Dreams: Mentoring Emerging Adults in their Search for Meaning, Purpose, and Faith* (San Francisco: Jossey-Bass, 2011).

2

ACT JUSTLY

Those who oppress the poor insult their Maker,
but those who are kind to the needy honor him.

—Proverbs 14:31

Justice is not a mere norm, but a fighting challenge, a rest-
less drive.

—Abraham Joshua Heschel

THE PSALMS OFFER a striking image of God as a *lover of justice*:

> Mighty King, lover of justice,
> you have established equity. (Ps 99:4)

We love justice not by devoting ourselves to an abstract principle or idea of justice, but by acting justly—by *doing* justice. To paraphrase a memorable line from Gerard Manley Hopkins:"the just person justices."[1] In regard to how we treat other people, we are what we do.

---

[1] "The just man justices" is the original line. Gerard Manley Hopkins, "As Kingfishers Catch Fire," in *Gerard Manley Hopkins: The Major Works* (Oxford: Oxford University Press, 1986), 129.

In this chapter I explore some ways that justice was understood by the prophets. These intense men possessed not only an acute awareness of injustice but a profound capacity to imagine more just and decent ways of being together in the world. They also had a unique way of seeing justice and mercy as integrally related. I also reflect on some of the affective and relational dimensions of the sense of justice, because callings often originate in the feelings of compassion and indignation that are evoked in our hearts by the unjust suffering of others. Along the way I lift up some exemplary people whose sense of personal vocation has been marked by a profound sense of justice.

THE PROPHETS AND JUSTICE

Two Hebrew words associated with justice, *mishpat* and *tsedakah,* are used over and over by the prophets. They are related but have somewhat different meanings. *Mishpat* coincides fairly well with our common understanding of justice as fair judgment and equitable treatment, giving each person his or her due punishment or reward.

Tsedakah, on the other hand, has to do with *righteousness,* which is a quality of personhood demonstrated by persons of integrity who value justice.[2] *Righteousness* is less tangible and harder to define than *justice,* but we certainly know it when we see it in people. *Tsedakah* is the root of *tzaddik,* the Hebrew word used to refer to a just or righteous person. Pope Francis, for example, is widely regarded as a just and righteous person not only by Catholics but by many non-Catholics and non-Christians because of his humility, his plainspoken advocacy for economic

---

[2] English renderings of these Hebrew words vary; I am following the spellings used by Abraham Joshua Heschel in *The Prophets* (New York: Harper Perennial, 1962).

and environmental justice, and his evident fondness for the poor. He embodies the qualities of the *tzaddik*.

The prophets spoke of justice and righteousness in conjunction with each other, sometimes within the same breath:

> But let justice [*mishpat*] roll down like waters,
>   And righteousness [*tsedakah*] like an ever-
>   flowing stream. (Am 5:24)

> Thus says the Lord: Act with justice [*mishpat*] and righteousness [*tsedekah*], and deliver from the hand of the oppressor anyone who has been robbed. (Jer 22:3)

Zechariah, Isaiah, and others also expanded the notion of justice to include protection of the *rights* of those in their society who were most vulnerable to being hurt and taken advantage of:

> Thus says the Lord of hosts: Render true judgments [*mishpat*], show kindness and mercy; do not oppress the widow, the orphan, the alien, or the poor. (Zec 7:9–10)

> Seek justice,
>   rescue the oppressed,
> defend the orphan,
>   plead for the widow. (Is 1:17)

Widows, orphans, immigrants, and the poor are mentioned so frequently by the prophets that they have been called the "quartet of the vulnerable."[3] It is not hard to think of a multitude of contemporary parallels to these vulnerable groups in the ancient world. Undocumented migrants, refugees, and asylum seekers

---

[3] Timothy Keller, *Generous Justice* (New York: Riverhead Books, 2010), 4.

are some of the first that come to mind. In the above passages I would prefer the word *immigrant* to *alien* because of the pejorative connotations of *alien* in the current debate over immigration in the United States (that is, referring to people as "illegal aliens").

As I write, controversies rage in the United States and Europe over whether migrants, refugees, and asylum seekers should have any rights to protection, refuge, or hospitality at all. Meanwhile, Central Americans attempting to cross the US border die from dehydration in the Arizona desert; Eritreans and other East Africans trying to reach Italy perish in rickety boats on the Mediterranean; desperate Middle Eastern people suffocate in the trucks of human smugglers in Europe; and Syrian children trying to get to Greece are drowned and wash back up onto the same beach they set out from. (Over 400,000 Syrians have been killed and as many as eleven million have fled their homes due to the catastrophic civil war in their homeland; of these, about seven million are internally displaced and over four million are refugees in the neighboring countries of Lebanon, Jordan, Iraq, Turkey, and beyond.)

The prophets were ever hopeful, but they were not optimistic about prospects for a sweeping breakthrough of God's justice and kindness any time soon. They knew the cries of the poor were likely to remain unheard because of stubborn human tendencies toward hard-heartedness and refusal to listen. The anguish of the poor always touches the heart of God, but more often than not it fails to register in enough human hearts to make a difference. Zechariah was disappointed:

> But they refused to listen and turned a stubborn shoulder,
> and stopped their ears in order not to hear. (Zec 7:11)

The prophets were acutely aware of injustice, of *what should not be so* in this world. They not only perceived it, they *felt* the appropriate human response to it. And they felt called to speak up about it. Consequently, by turns, their hearts were compassionate and tender, indignant and furious, sorrowful and grief-stricken. Just listen to Jeremiah:

> For the hurt of my poor people I am hurt,
>   I mourn, and dismay has taken hold of me.
>
> Is there no balm in Gilead?
>   Is there no physician there?
> Why then has the health of my poor people
>   not been restored?
> O that my head were a spring of water,
>   and my eyes a fountain of tears,
> So that I might weep day and night
>   for the slain of my poor people! (Jer 8:21–
>   9:1)

The prophets seemed to have a capacity to feel what society-at-large was trying *not* to feel. In their own consciousness they broke through the kind of defensive denial that results in collective apathy, numbness, and complacency about things that should provoke shame, sorrow, or outrage.[4] In their own hearts they experienced the heartache and heartbreak of God.

> My anguish, my anguish! I writhe in pain!
>   Oh, the walls of my heart!
> My heart is beating wildly;
>   I cannot keep silent. (Jer 4:19)

Jeremiah is not being hysterical or indulging in self-pity. He is experiencing the distress of God! And he is hoping that *saying*

---

[4] See Walter Brueggemann's excellent chapter "Prophetic Criticizing and the Embrace of Pathos," in *The Prophetic Imagination*, 2nd ed. (Minneapolis, MN: Fortress Press, 2001), 39–58.

something about it will awaken others from their lethargic sleep. "He has only the hope," says Brueggemann, "that the ache of God will penetrate the numbness of history."[5]

There is a way that each of us is called to cultivate a kind of prophetic consciousness in our own life and times. This requires, first of all, a personal confrontation with our own tendencies toward numbness, apathy, indifference, and complacency—with anything that tends to mute or constrain the response of our own hearts to suffering and injustice.

There are many ways to become aware of such things. We might, for example, feel moved by a news story about the plight of a particular group of people, but then notice how quickly we are able to simply turn off our feelings and move on to thinking about something else. On the one hand, this is an understandable self-protective mechanism that helps us to cope with feelings of helplessness and hopelessness about the sheer magnitude and complexity of the world's problems. But if this becomes a habitual way of being, our horizons get narrower and narrower, and our hearts begin to shrink. We become less able to see and hear and feel the world around us. Jesus, paraphrasing the prophet Isaiah before him, seemed exasperated and pained at the degree to which people could become so closed and shut down:

With them indeed is fulfilled the prophecy of Isaiah that says:

"You will listen, but never understand,
    and you will indeed look, but never perceive.
For this people's heart has grown dull,
    and their ears are hard of hearing,
        and they have shut their eyes;

---

[5] Ibid., 55.

so that they might not look with their
eyes,
and listen with their ears,
and understand with their heart and turn—
and I would heal them." (Mt 13:14–15; cf.
Is 6:9–10)

Careful reflection on an uneasy conscience is another path to prophetic consciousness. Sometimes certain situations and issues are not so easy to put out of our minds; they weigh on us, nag at us, intrude upon our efforts to go about business as usual. The US invasion and occupation of Iraq had this effect upon me for years. When I allowed myself to think about it, the sheer waste and destructiveness of the whole thing made me ashamed and depressed and angry. I began to see such feelings as the emotional echoes of the inner voice of conscience. Through them, my conscience was not only speaking within me, but it was urging me to give voice to my inner aversion to the war through public opposition and dissent.

I came to believe that keeping silent about the war would amount to a betrayal of my conscience. I felt called to speak up about it. This prompted a variety of modest efforts on my part to oppose the war through writing, teaching, attending protests, and years of phone calls and letters to public officials and newspapers. Many people did much more, sometimes at considerable personal cost, including participation in acts of civil disobedience resulting in arrest. Some friends from my church kept a weekly rush-hour vigil at a busy Chicago intersection for years. They held signs with photos of Iraqi children to represent all the innocents who were needlessly put in harm's way by American belligerence and the relentless and bloody mayhem it had set in motion.

I also had an uneasy conscience about the seemingly endless cascade of revelations that the United States had engaged in the widespread and systematic practice of torture in the years following the 9/11 terrorist attacks.[6] As a citizen, and as a psychologist who has worked with survivors of torture for many years, I found this appalling. I was particularly embarrassed by reports that psychologists had been directly involved in guiding and monitoring torture sessions at places like the Guantanamo Bay prison camp, which has become a global symbol of injustice and cruelty. Psychological knowledge and skills are meant to be used for healing, not for breaking people down!

Incredibly, after all this, in 2005 the leadership of the American Psychological Association (APA) still felt moved to give its official blessing to the ongoing involvement of psychologists in so-called enhanced interrogations with detainees in the so-called War on Terrorism. I joined other concerned psychologists in efforts to challenge and pressure the APA leadership to repent and change its position. Many of us withheld our professional dues and many, including me, eventually resigned in protest. The official response to conscientious dissent was persistent stonewalling, cover-up, and self-serving "spin," all of which apparently served to protect financially lucrative and politically advantageous connections among the APA, the Pentagon, and the Central Intelligence Agency. Finally, over a decade later, there have been some belated expressions of regret and moves toward accountability.[7]

> Everyone deals falsely.
> They have treated the wound of my people
>   carelessly,

---

[6] See John Neafsey, "The Scandal of Torture," chap. 2, in *Crucified People: The Suffering of the Tortured in Today's World,* (Maryknoll, NY: Orbis Books, 2014).

[7] See James Risen, "Outside Psychologists Shielded US Torture Program, Report Finds," *New York Times,* July 10, 2015. See also the accompanying link to "Psychologists and Enhanced Interrogation," which includes the full 542–page report (known as the Hoffman Report) of an independent investigation of the American Psychological Association, national security interrogations, and torture.

saying "Peace, peace,"
when there is no peace. (Jer 6:13–14)

Offering prophetic criticism is an important dimension of the prophet's calling. The point is to cut through the phony pretense of peace "when there is no peace." Sometimes the prophets delivered their criticism in a tone of grief and lament:

My joy is gone, grief is upon me,
my heart is sick. (Jer 8:18).[8]

It could also be accompanied by biting judgment and indignation. The prophets could be as harsh in their denunciation of hypocrisy and wickedness in high places as they were kind to the poor.

Your wealthy are full of violence;
your inhabitants speak lies
with tongues of deceit in their mouths. (Mi
6:12)

Prophetic criticism can provoke defensiveness and hostility in those who are on the receiving end of it. They would prefer that the prophet tone it down, or go away. They would rather not hear about it.

They hate the one who reproves in the gate,
and they abhor the one who speaks the truth.
(Am 5:10)

Israel cries,

---

[8] See Brueggemann, *The Prophetic Imagination*: "I believe that grief and mourning, that crying in pathos, is the ultimate form of criticism" (46).

"The prophet is a fool,
    the man of the spirit is mad!" (Hos 9:7)

[They] say to the seers, "Do not see";
    and to the prophets, "Do not prophesy to us
        what is right";
speak to us smooth things,
    prophesy illusions. (Is 30:10)

The prophet is more than a social critic or a scold. After confronting the mess that has been made, the crucial prophetic task is to imagine or envision something new and different: the world as it *could* be or *should* be. *It does not have to be like this; there is another way.* Brueggemann calls this *prophetic imagination.* The prophets of ancient Israel did not come up with political platforms or mission statements or ten-point action plans. They were visionaries and poets, leaving the details and implementation to others. Their gift was to offer evocative and inspiring images of alternative worlds:

They shall beat their swords into plowshares,
    and their spears into pruning hooks;
nation shall not lift sword against nation,
    neither shall they learn war any more. (Mi 4:3;
        cf. Is 2:4)

The wolf shall lie down with the lamb,
    the leopard shall lie down with the kid,
the calf and the lion and the fatling together,
    and a little child shall lead them. (Is 11:6)

The breakthrough of such a peaceable kingdom always begins quite humbly in movements of the human heart. Numb, unresponsive hearts are awakened and quickened. Hearts change, people change.

> A new heart I will give you, and a new spirit I will put within you; and I will remove from your body the heart of stone and give you a heart of flesh. (Ez 36:26)

The new heart, the "heart of flesh" of which Ezekiel speaks, is a responsive heart, an open heart. It is a heart capable of being moved by injustice and suffering—and of moving us to *do* something about it.

JUST MERCY

Justice and mercy are integrally related. The prophets often spoke of justice in conjunction with another Hebrew word, *hesed,* which means "kindness" or "mercy." Micah asks us not only to "do justice" *(mishpat)* but to "love kindness" *(hesed)*. Zechariah urges us to "render true judgments" *(mishpat)* and to "show kindness and mercy" *(hesed)*.

The spiritual heart of the matter is revealed in a lovely line spoken by Portia in Shakespeare's *The Merchant of Venice*: "And earthly power doth then show likest God's when mercy seasons justice." In today's English, her words might read something like: Justice done with mercy best reflects how God does things. Judgment is tempered and softened by mercy; justice administered with kindness is humanized, personalized. Abraham Joshua Heschel writes:

> Justice exists in relation to a person, and is something done by a person. An act of injustice is condemned not because the law is broken, but because a person has been hurt. A person is a being whose anguish may reach the heart of God.[9]

---

[9] Heschel, *The Prophets,* 276.

For the prophets, justice was not blind or objective or impartial. It was *personal*. The prophets thought we *should* be partial to people who never seem to get a break, who always have the deck stacked against them—not only in the justice system but in life. "Justice was not equal justice," explains Heschel, "but a bias in favor of the poor. Justice always leaned toward mercy for the widows and the orphans."[10] The prophets took sides, embodying in ancient times what twentieth-century liberation theologians called the "preferential option for the poor."

> "How long will you judge unjustly
>   and show partiality to the wicked?
> Give justice to the weak and the orphan;
>   Maintain the right of the lowly and the destitute. (Ps 82:2–3)

Sadly, the criminal justice system in the United States often seems to operate with a kind of blind, impersonal, systemic bias against the poor. This is especially the case for people of color from backgrounds of poverty, who are often subject to unacknowledged presumptions that persons with black or brown skin are dangerous and guilty. Such presumptions can have an adverse influence on every stage of the legal process, from racial profiling in the initial contact with police through racial bias in trial and sentencing. On top of this, for the simple reason that they don't have money, poor people in trouble are more likely to have inadequate or incompetent legal help in their dealings with the frustrating and confusing bureaucracy of the criminal justice system.

"We have a system of justice in this country," says Bryan Stevenson, "that treats you much better if you're rich and guilty

---

[10] Ibid., 257.

than if you're poor and innocent."[11] Stevenson is the founder of the Equal Justice Initiative, an Alabama-based program whose mission is to provide legal representation and advocacy for poor people who have gotten into serious trouble. Since its founding in 1989, the Equal Justice Initiative has devoted special attention to two uniquely vulnerable populations: prisoners condemned to death by execution (including a significant number who are actually innocent), and children who have been sentenced to life imprisonment without the possibility of parole—otherwise known as "death in prison." The program has also challenged the alarming trend toward mass incarceration of people for nonviolent crimes; over the last forty years the US prison population has increased from 300,000 to 2.3 million. Not surprisingly, the prisoners are disproportionately poor, African American, and male.

Stevenson is also the author of a moving memoir titled *Just Mercy: A Story of Justice and Redemption*.[12] The book is full of poignant stories of the people Stevenson and his colleagues are trying to help, stories that put human faces and personal narratives to those who would otherwise be counted only as tragic and unfortunate statistics. It is also the inspiring story of Stevenson's personal discovery of his own calling, which he has found in a firm commitment to work for justice for the incarcerated and condemned and in an ever-deepening resolve to challenge systemic bias against the poor and people of color in the criminal justice system.

Just Mercy begins with Stevenson's profoundly formative experience as a young law student during a summer internship in the early 1980s with the Southern Prisoners Defense Committee, an Atlanta-based legal assistance program for death-row prisoners

---

[11] Bryan Stevenson, "We Need to Talk about an Injustice" (March 2012), video on http://www.ted.com.

[12] Bryan Stevenson, *Just Mercy: A Story of Justice and Redemption* (New York: Spiegel and Grau, 2014).

throughout the South. He distinctly recalls the provocative words of an important early mentor at the program: "Bryan, capital punishment means 'them without the capital get the punishment.'"[13] Stevenson's moving and unsettling encounters with death-row prisoners that summer affected him deeply and had a profound impact on the trajectory of the rest of his life:

> I finished my internship committed to helping the death row prisoners I had met that month. Proximity to the condemned and incarcerated made the question of each person's humanity more urgent and meaningful, including my own. I went back to law school with an intense desire to understand the laws that sanctioned the death penalty and extreme punishments. . . . I plunged deeply into the sociology of race, poverty, and power. Law school had seemed abstract and disconnected before, but after meeting the desperate and condemned, it all became relevant and critically important.[14]

Beyond his professional interests and aspirations Stevenson's experiences with prisoners also led to important personal insights into himself and his own history. Although he had never been in trouble and had not suffered the kind of extreme trauma and deprivation that many of his clients have experienced, he certainly has known injustice by virtue of the fact that he grew up as an African American in a poor, racially segregated area of Delaware in the 1960s. "The more I reflected on the experience," he writes, "the more I recognized that I had been struggling my whole life with the question of how and why people are treated unfairly." His personal experience of growing up in a community that had to contend with injustice on a day-to-day basis seemed

---

[13] Ibid., 6.
[14] Ibid., 13.

to be the very thing that enabled him to identify and connect with people caught up in an unjust system. "Proximity to the condemned, to people unfairly judged; that was what guided me back to something that felt like home."[15]

Becoming involved with desperate people can evoke deep feelings in those who take the risk of getting close to them: sorrow, anger, helplessness, hopelessness, frustration, and despair. Stevenson recalls how he once became so exasperated by the inequities of the criminal justice system for young African Americans that he drafted a legal motion on behalf of one of his clients titled "Motion to Try My Poor, Fourteen-Year-Old Black Male Client Like a Privileged, White, Seventy-Five-Year-Old Corporate Executive."[16] Although the judge was annoyed with him for introducing issues of race, poverty, and privilege to the case, Stevenson was becoming increasingly convinced that such things often seemed to determine the fate of the people he was trying to help.

Stevenson also came to appreciate how a little mercy could make a profound difference in the lives of the people he serves, even for those guilty of shocking crimes that had destroyed lives—including their own. "Proximity has taught me some basic and humbling truths," he writes, "including this vital lesson: *Each of us is more than the worst thing we've ever done.*"[17] On an emotional and spiritual level the experience of being regarded with mercy can provide at least some relief from debilitating feelings of shame and self-loathing for past sins. On a practical level, cultivating a more merciful understanding of clients can also be an effective legal tool:

> In all death penalty cases, spending time with clients is important. Developing the trust of clients is not only

---

[15] Ibid., 13–14.

[16] Stevenson, "We Need to Talk about an Injustice."

[17] Stevenson, *Just Mercy*, 18.

necessary to manage the complexities of the litigation and deal with the stress of a potential execution; it's also key to effective advocacy. A client's life often depends on his lawyer's ability to create a mitigation narrative that contextualizes his poor decisions or violent behavior. Uncovering things about someone's background that no one has previously discovered—things that might be hard to discuss but are critically important—requires trust.[18]

A *mitigation narrative* is a story that offers a less harsh, more compassionate way of understanding how and why things seem to have gone so wrong. Instead of narrowly judging or defining people by the worst thing they have ever done, it broadens the picture by taking important factors in their personal background and history into account. Through patient listening, cultivation of trust, and a careful and thorough review of all available records and evidence, it is possible to see people's crimes in the context of their complex and often tragic lives: sexual or physical abuse in childhood, neglect or abandonment, intellectual disability, untreated mental illness or substance abuse, post-traumatic stress—the sad list goes on and on. Crimes are not excused or condoned, but they become understandable when the broken individuals who committed them are regarded with a measure of mercy.

On a fundamental human level we are *all* broken, and we all need mercy. "We have all hurt someone and have been hurt," says Stevenson. "We all share the condition of brokenness even if our brokenness is not equivalent."[19] Paradoxically, it is our own brokenness that helps us to recognize and *feel* our common humanity with others—even with people from backgrounds very different from our own.

---

[18] Ibid., 104.
[19] Ibid.. 289.

WE ARE ALL RELATED

During certain ritual ceremonies of the Native American peoples of the Great Plains it is customary for participants to exclaim, "We are all related!" In the Lakota Sioux language the expression is "Mitakuye oyasin!"[20] They are referring here to something deeper and more expansive than family or tribal kinship. In Native American spirituality the sense of underlying connection and relatedness extends beyond the personal circle to all living beings, human and nonhuman (animals, birds, trees, plants, fish, insects), and the whole of the natural world. What is being felt and affirmed is "the mysterious interrelatedness of all that is."[21]

We can consider the call to justice in similar affective and relational terms. These center around the quality of our personhood in relation to others. Our sense of justice is grounded in a recognition of our common humanity and solidarity, a sense of brotherhood or sisterhood with people in need or trouble. In solidarity with others we become more deeply and authentically human. We are put in touch with our capacity to be moved by suffering, to be upset by unjust situations that are causing hurt and deprivation, to identify with the yearnings and aspirations of those who are oppressed by one form of injustice or another. Callings to compassionate service and just action have their origin in such feelings and the inclinations that accompany them. From this perspective vocation is not only about *me* and my personal fulfillment, but about *us* and the common good.

This way of thinking is beautifully exemplified by the African concept of *ubuntu*, which is analogous to *tsedakah* in the Jewish tradition. *Ubuntu* is a word from the Nguni language group

---

[20] *Mitakuye oyasin* has been translated into English variously as "All my relatives" or "All my relations" or "We are all related."

[21] Joseph Epes Brown, *The Spiritual Legacy of the American Indian* (Bloomington, IN: World Wisdom, 2007), 39–40.

in southern Africa. Archbishop Desmond Tutu says this about *ubuntu*:

> *Ubuntu* is very difficult to render into a Western language. It speaks of the very essence of being human. When we want to give high praise to someone we say "*Yu u nobuntu*"; "Hey, so-and-so has *ubuntu*." Then you are generous, you are hospitable, you are friendly and caring and compassionate. You share what you have. It is to say, "My humanity is caught up, inextricably bound up, in yours." We belong in a bundle of life. We say "A person is a person through other persons." . . . A person with *ubuntu* is open and available to others, affirming of others, does not feel threatened that others are able and good, for he or she has a proper self-assurance that comes from knowing that he or she belongs in a greater whole and is diminished when others are humiliated or diminished, when others are tortured and oppressed, or treated as if they were less than who they are.[22]

With this sense of connection and solidarity with others comes a sense of responsibility for them. The person with *ubuntu* is moved to compassion and indignation by unjust suffering—and is inclined to do something about it. There is a beautiful example from the life of Dr. Martin Luther King, Jr., a person who can surely be regarded as having possessed *ubuntu* in abundance.

In early April 1963, in response to ongoing reports of vicious racism and officially sanctioned segregation in Birmingham, Alabama, Dr. King and his colleagues from the Southern Christian Leadership Conference made a decision to go to Birmingham to bring the pressure of nonviolent direct action and national media attention to bear on the situation there. Initially, there

---

[22] Desmond Tutu, *No Future without Forgiveness* (New York: Doubleday, 1999), 31.

was considerable resistance to King's presence in Birmingham, including among some sectors of the African American community. Some had concerns that King was an "outside agitator" or troublemaker who had no business being there. Over the course of the next month or so over a thousand demonstrators were arrested and detained (including many elementary, high school, and college students), to the point that the city jails were filled beyond capacity. News photos and video footage of Birmingham police using high-pressure fire hoses and attack dogs on demonstrators shocked the conscience of the nation.

On April 12, which happened to be Good Friday, Dr. King and his colleagues decided to subject themselves to arrest by violating a court injunction that had been hastily issued to crack down on public protests of any sort. King was immediately arrested, after which the authorities took the gratuitous punitive measure of putting him into solitary confinement at the Birmingham Jail. Initially, he was not even permitted to meet with his lawyer or make a phone call to his wife.

By Easter Sunday, after the intervention of both Attorney General Robert Kennedy and President John F. Kennedy, Dr. King was transferred to a regular cell. His lawyer gave him a newspaper that contained an editorial by eight moderate white ministers from Alabama who expressed concern about the "unwise and untimely" demonstrations being fomented by outside agitators and who counseled "patience" on the part of black citizens. Personally hurt and incensed, King began composing a response on the margins of the newspaper that would become, over the course of the following week before his release, his famous "Letter from Birmingham City Jail." In the letter he carefully explained the various reasons he had chosen to become involved in this local struggle. "I am in Birmingham," he wrote, "because injustice is here." His most eloquent and persuasive rationale for being there, though, was a profound expression of the essence of *ubuntu:*

Moreover, I am cognizant of the interrelatedness of all communities and states. I cannot sit idly by in Atlanta and not be concerned about what happens in Birmingham. Injustice anywhere is a threat to justice everywhere. Whatever affects one directly affects all indirectly. We are caught in an inescapable network of mutuality, tied in a single garment of destiny.[23]

We could say that the person with *ubuntu* feels a calling to act justly, love tenderly, and walk humbly because the well-being of others *depends* upon it. Conducting ourselves with justice, kindness, and humility always begins, of course, with how we treat our loved ones and people in the circle of our everyday lives. When we consider ourselves as citizens of the wider world, though, the calling extends beyond our personal circle to an ever-expanding network of connection and solidarity with people both far and near. We are all related!

BEARING WITNESS

It is hard to forget the haunting image of James Foley in an orange jumpsuit kneeling beside his executioner in the bleak landscape of the Syrian desert in August 2014. After ISIS released its "Message to America" video of Foley's beheading, countless people around the world came to know about his unspeakably cruel death. Sadly, not so many know about his beautiful life or his inspired calling to bear witness to the sufferings of innocent people caught in the crossfire of war in the Middle East.

I never had the honor of knowing James Foley personally. But there was something about his story that got to me, that made

---

[23] Dr. Martin Luther King, Jr., "Letter from Birmingham City Jail," in *A Testament of Hope: The Essential Writings and Speeches of Martin Luther King, Jr.*, ed. James M. Washington (New York: HarperCollins, 2003 <1986>), 289–302.

me want to learn more about how a person like Foley could end up in such a situation. On the occasion of what would have been Foley's forty-first birthday (October 18, 2014), I attended a moving memorial mass and celebration of his life at his family's home church in Rochester, New Hampshire. Hundreds joined the Foley family for this poignant occasion at Our Lady of the Holy Rosary Church. A diverse array of friends and colleagues from different eras of his life came from near and far to honor the man they affectionately knew as "Jim" or "Jimmy."

People who knew Foley consistently made note of his kindness and generosity, his bold and adventuresome spirit, his charming manner, his stunning good looks, and his remarkable capacity to empathize and connect with people—especially those from backgrounds very different from his own. "Everybody, everywhere, takes a liking to Jim as soon as they meet him," writes Clare Morgana Gillis, a journalist colleague who had been imprisoned along with Foley in Libya for forty-four days in 2011.[24] (Ms. Gillis was at the memorial in Rochester, having traveled all the way from the Middle East to honor her friend.)

Certain snapshots of Foley that reveal his character stand out. There was the idealistic young graduate of Marquette University who really took the Jesuit ideal of being a "person for others" to heart; after graduation he went on to teach poor kids in Phoenix with Teach for America and later juvenile inmates at the Cook County Jail in Chicago. After a career change in his thirties, he became the courageous photojournalist reporting from hazardous places like Iraq, Afghanistan, Libya, and Syria. During his 2011 captivity in Libya there was the poignant image of Foley seeking consolation in that dark time through praying the Rosary (in the absence of beads, he used his knuckles to keep count of the Hail Marys). Not long before he was captured in Syria there

---

[24] Claire Morgana Gillis, "My Friend James Foley," *Syria Deeply* (blog), May 1, 2013.

was a harrowing video report he filmed and narrated from a hospital in Aleppo about all of the innocent men, women, and children who were being injured in the bloody mayhem of the Syrian civil war. Pained by the lack of resources to care for the injured, Foley personally organized a campaign to raise money to purchase an ambulance for Dar al-Shifa Hospital in Aleppo. There are also moving reports from a number of fellow hostages of Foley's consistent kindness and generosity of spirit during his final captivity in Syria.[25]

Late in his Syrian captivity, when he seemed to know that he would not make it out alive, there was a heartbreakingly tender letter to his family and loved ones. Because no written communication was permitted, Foley's message was memorized by a fellow hostage who was about to be released; it was later delivered verbally over the phone to his mother:

> "I remember going to the Mall with Dad, a very long bike ride with Mom. I remember so many great family times that take me away from this prison. Dreams of family and friends take me away and happiness fills my heart. . . .
>
> "I know you are thinking of me and praying for me. And I am so thankful. I feel you all especially when I pray. I pray for you to stay strong and to believe. I really feel I can touch you even in this darkness when I pray."[26]

Particularly moving was a televised press conference shortly after Foley's death with his grief-stricken parents, John and Diane Foley. Remarkably dignified and articulate, Mr. and Mrs. Foley

---

[25] Several former hostages who came to know Foley during his Syrian captivity are interviewed in a powerful documentary entitled *Jim: The James Foley Story*, directed by Brian Oakes (HBO Documentary Films), television premiere February 6, 2016.

[26] See http://www.jamesfoleyfoundation.org for the full text of "Jim's Last Letter."

honestly acknowledged their reservations about their son's work in the Middle East—especially after his captivity in Libya. Some of the family had tried to talk him out of going back, hoping he could find a less hazardous way to be true to his conscience. But his parents also recalled how passionately he spoke of his sense of *vocation* as a journalist, his feeling that *someone* needed to document stories and images of the suffering of innocent people for a world that would otherwise not know what they were going through. Mr. Foley likened his son's attitude to that of firefighters who feel they *must* go back into a burning building if there are people inside who need help. "We have never been prouder of our son Jim," said his mother. "He gave his life trying to expose the world to the suffering of the Syrian people."[27]

Foley was a man of action. "He's always been willing to step into a zone where no one else wants to go," wrote his friend Sarah Fang for Teach for America. "Jim feels that society needs reporters willing to bear witness and report back the facts of history-in-the-making." Fr. Paul Gousse, the pastor of his family's church, recalls poignantly what Foley told him prior to his final trip to Syria: "The world needs to know the plight of the little people who are walked upon like grass."[28] It seems he found it hard to resist inner promptings that led him to places where he could witness firsthand what was happening to the kind of people Jesus referred to as "the least of these."

Some fellow hostages who were released have reported that Foley appeared to have undergone a conversion to Islam some time during his final captivity.[29] It is natural to suspect the

[27] Diane Foley, quoted in Uri Friedman, "James Foley and the Last Journalists in Syria," *The Atlantic*, August 19, 2014.

[28] See Jonathan Mahler, "James Foley: He Risked Everything to Get Closer," in a collection of articles entitled "The Lives They Lived: Remembering Some of Those We Lost This Year," *New York Times Magazine*, December 23, 2014.

[29] See Rukmini Callimachi, "The Horror before the Beheadings," *New York Times*, October 25, 2014. See also Jim Yardley, "Debating a Change of Faith under Captivity," *New York Times*, February 21, 2015.

authenticity of a conversion under such circumstances, because fellow prisoners have also said that Foley was cruelly tortured by his captors on numerous occasions. It is impossible to know what the practice of Muslim prayer meant for him in this situation. It may have been some comfort in a dark time, just as praying the Rosary had provided consolation in his earlier captivity.

When asked about her son and Islam, Mrs. Foley responded, "Only God and Jim know what was going on inside his heart."[30] We can be certain, though, that James Foley was a just man with a tender heart for people in trouble. And we can also be quite sure that God, by whatever name, knows this too.

VOICE IN THE WILDERNESS

Certain prophetic people are called to *resistance*. For some, this becomes a way of life. They refuse to go along, they won't cooperate; through words or actions they say, "No, not in my name." Sometimes they make trouble; sometimes they get into trouble. They would rather go to jail than compromise their conscience.

Not long ago I had the privilege of talking with Kathy Kelly, a peace activist from Chicago. We visited for a few hours in my office at the Kovler Center, a treatment center for immigrant survivors of torture in the Rogers Park neighborhood, which is not far from where she lives. Kathy has been imprisoned over sixty times for reasons of conscience, including four times in US federal prisons. She has lost count of how many times she has been locked up in municipal or county jails. "If jailbirds were listed in an avian guide," one reporter quipped, "Kathy Kelly would rate a special entry for 'dove.'"[31]

---

[30] Mrs. Foley, quoted in James Carroll, "God Was James Foley's Witness," *Boston Globe,* February 27, 2015.

[31] Don Terry, "The Peace Warrior," *Chicago Tribune Magazine*, October 17, 2004, 14.

Although Kathy has a larger-than-life reputation, in person she is not an imposing presence at all. Now sixty-two, she is a petite woman, not much more than five feet tall, with long, tousled, curly hair. Though she has a long history of remarkable audacity in confronting the powers that be, her personal warmth and courtesy are quite disarming. She has a gentle smile and an Irish twinkle in her kind eyes.

Kathy's prison record and the country stamps on her passport will forever keep her on the watch list of the FBI and the Department of Homeland Security. For decades she has been a frequent visitor to some of the world's most dangerous war zones, including Bosnia, Nicaragua, the West Bank and Gaza, Iraq, and Afghanistan. In March 2003, in solidarity with Iraqi people who couldn't escape the bombs, she and her companions stayed in a small hotel in Baghdad through the entire US "Shock and Awe" bombing campaign. And, because of her principled opposition to government use of tax dollars to pay for war and preparation for war, she has refused to pay taxes for over thirty years. Instead, she chooses to keep her income below the minimum taxable level, live simply, and own nothing.

Her exploits have brought her a certain notoriety in activist circles. Rather in awe of her, one young interviewer blurted out, "Kathy, the only way I can really describe you is . . . a *total bad-ass!*"[32] There really is a kind of audacity, even *effrontery*, about some of the things she has done over the years. Between 1996 and 2003, in open and deliberate violation of UN and US economic sanctions, she traveled to Iraq twenty-six times to deliver medicine and food and toys for children with a group she co-founded called Voices in the Wilderness. To Kathy, breaking a few laws seemed insignificant when weighed against the lives of the

---

[32] Interview by Luke Rudkowski (of WeAreChange), "True Resistance: Kathy Kelly, 60–Years-Old with 60 Arrests," video, September 10, 2013, http://www.youtube.com/watch?v=QefzphHFmZk.

more than 500,000 Iraqi children who died during over a decade of punitive sanctions.[33] "We're governed by compassion," she explained, "not by laws that pitilessly murder innocent children."[34] She likened sanctions to a modern form of child sacrifice that is practiced in political games between nations.

Kathy lives in a Chicago apartment that served as the home base for Voices in The Wilderness. In 2005, that organization evolved into Voices for Creative Nonviolence. The earlier group, a loose coalition of like-minded peace and justice activists, came into being in the early 1990s to oppose sanctions against Iraq. Sadly, it eventually became necessary to shift its mission to opposing the US invasion and occupation. The current group, some of whose members live with Kathy, has a number of priorities, including consciousness raising about the impact of ongoing war on the civilian population of Afghanistan and opposition to US use of drone warfare in Afghanistan, Pakistan, Yemen, Somalia, and other places.

A Chicago native, Kathy travels frequently for speaking engagements and international solidarity work (she currently spends a lot of time in Afghanistan), and she is also sometimes away for prison time. Most recently, in early 2015, she served three months in federal prison for trespassing at Whiteman Air Force Base in Missouri, a facility that serves as a remote command and control center for targeted drone attacks in Afghanistan. On June 1, 2014, she walked onto the base carrying only a loaf of bread and a letter to the commanding officer; her stated intent was "breaking bread" and having a talk with him. The letter, citing statistics that US drones kill an estimated twenty-eight innocent civilians for each suspected enemy combatant, asked a

---

[33] Barbara Crossette, "Iraq Sanctions Kill Children, UN Reports," *New York Times,* December 30, 1995.

[34] See Kathy Kelly, "Banning Child Sacrifice: A Difficult Choice?" in *Other Lands Have Dreams: From Baghdad to Pekin Prison* (Petrolia, CA: Counterpunch, 2005), 35–39.

pointed question: How many people in Afghanistan were killed by Whiteman Air Force Base today? At her sentencing hearing the military prosecutor told the judge, "Your honor, Ms. Kelly is in grave need of rehabilitation." Looking back, Kathy is unrepentant: "I certainly don't think I did anything wrong," she says. "I'm proud of what I did. . . . I think it's our *policy* that's in grave need of rehabilitation."[35]

Kelly's past affiliation with a group called Voices in the Wilderness may conjure up images of a fiery, uncompromising prophet like John the Baptist. And there is certainly something of this prophetic fire in her. Indeed, much of what Kathy says and does is like "the voice of one crying in the wilderness" (Mk 1:2). But there is also a sincerity and sweetness of spirit about her that are reminiscent of Francis of Assisi. With her, I had the distinct sense of being in the presence of someone without guile. She struck me as the kind of person who, like Francis during the Crusades, might decide to go and have a talk with the sultan about making peace. She has also been compared to Dorothy Day, a woman whose life embodied similar commitments to the works of mercy and the struggle for peace and justice.

One of the most striking things about Kathy is her idealism, which seems to center around a few core principles or beliefs. She once wrote:

One of the greatest gifts in life is to find a few beliefs that you can declare with passion and then have the freedom to act on them. For me, those beliefs are quite simple: that nonviolence and pacifism can change the world, that the poor should be society's greatest priority, that people

---

[35] Kathy Kelly, quoted in Medea Benjamin, "Federal Prison Sentence Begins for Anti-Drone Activist," *Common Dreams* website, January 22, 2015. See also Ken Butigan, "Kathy Kelly Sentenced to Three Months in Prison for Anti-Drone Action," *Pace e Bene* website, December 9, 2014.

should love their enemies, and that actions should follow conviction, regardless of inconvenience.[36]

"Regardless of inconvenience" is quite a phrase. At sentencing hearings I suspect that most judges do not consult with defendants to see when jail time might be most convenient for them!

Kathy is also a firm believer in the idea that where we stand determines what we see. "We need to keep one foot firmly planted amid those bearing the consequences of war and injustice," she says, "and the other foot just as firmly planted amid those trying to resist it."[37] She travels to war zones so that she can see how things look and feel from the vantage point of those who are under the gun. While she is there, she gathers stories about the suffering of the innocent that she shares with anyone who will listen. She spends most of the rest of her time with those who are interested in hearing such stories: peacemakers and small communities of resistance, the kind of people who are willing to *make* a little trouble and sometimes maybe *get into* a little trouble for the sake of peace and justice.

Being a person who is consistently preoccupied with my own convenience, and also being a psychologist, I found myself wondering about the personal emotional toll of such a life, the "inconvenience" of prison, the cumulative effects of witnessing so much trauma and pain for so many years. In her writings Kathy is sometimes quite transparent about her feelings: "I felt sad and shattered when we left Iraq," she wrote after a particularly painful and disappointing visit during the period of sanctions. Facing the threat of prosecution on her return to the United States, there was a need to reassure herself of the basic rightness of what she was doing: "I know that our efforts to be voices in the wilder-

---

[36] Kelly, *Other Lands Have Dreams*, 17.
[37] Kathy Kelly, personal communication, November 6, 2015.

ness aren't criminal."[38] Some years later she felt a great sense of sorrow and disappointment at the onset of the Iraq War. "We almost stopped a war," she said wistfully to me, seeming to take some consolation in the memory of worldwide antiwar efforts to oppose those who were hell-bent on war.

Kathy has also wrestled with anger. She says she tries to contain and restrain inclinations to be self-righteous or "shrill" in her tone or speech. She sees anger as a source of energy that can be harnessed to motivate further nonviolent efforts.

> I believe we can channel our anger, our disappointment, our frustration, and our rage into the kind of energy that will champion nonviolent resistance to the works of war, and an ever-deepening desire for the works of mercy.[39]

In March 2003, in a small Baghdad hotel on the Tigris River, Kathy and her "peace team" companions felt a mounting sense of tension and suspense as they waited for the "Shock and Awe" bombardment to begin. "I felt dismay, deep sadness, anger," she wrote as the bombs began to fall, "but also a familiar sense of intense determination not to let the bombs have the last word."[40] After several days of ear-splitting, gut-wrenching blasts, she posted an essay titled "Angry, Very Angry":

> Yes, we are angry, very angry, and yet we feel deep responsibility to further the nonviolent antiwar efforts burgeoning in cities and towns throughout the world. We can direct our anger toward clear confrontation, controlling it so that we won't explode in reactionary rage, but rather draw the

---

[38] Kelly, *Other Lands Have Dreams*, 45.
[39] Ibid., 68.
[40] Ibid., 60.

sympathies of people toward the plight of innocent people here who never wanted to attack the United States, who wonder, even as the bombs terrify them, why they can't live as brothers and sisters with people in America.[41]

Kathy is a remarkably resilient person. Though she has experienced inner states that resemble symptoms of post-traumatic stress, she seems to have developed her own ways of working with such feelings so that they do not compromise her emotional health or work. Interestingly, she finds that telling stories of trauma through her talks and writing seems to help her to work through her own trauma. This is not why she does it, but she has discovered that raising consciousness through storytelling is also therapeutic for her. Even so, she says must be careful not to "retraumatize" herself in the telling of painful things that she has witnessed or experienced.

Also crucial is the network of mutual support and solidarity that Kathy has developed with a remarkably diverse community of people around the world. "I feel very grateful," she says, "because I've had the opportunity to meet the finest people in the world."[42] These include her companions in resistance, other women inmates she has come to know in prison, undersupplied Iraqi doctors and medical personnel she came to know during the sanctions, young Afghan peace volunteers she is now working with in Kabul, and so many others. Kathy says she "catches courage" from them.[43]

Kathy thinks she will eventually slow down a bit, "maybe travel less and write more." For now, though, she is keeping at it. At one point I asked, "What keeps you going?" She recalled the words of an activist friend who once offered this observation:

---

[41] Ibid., 67.

[42] Kelly, personal communication, November 6, 2015.

[43] Ibid.

"The real reason you do what you do, Kathy, is that you've *fallen in love*—you're *always* falling in love." With me, she was quick to qualify this, seeming concerned not to sentimentalize or romanticize her work. Nevertheless, it seems that her friend was on to something. One does not take such risks or make such sacrifices for the sake of principle alone. I thought of the well-known words usually attributed to Jesuit Pedro Arrupe:

> What you are in love with, what seizes your imagination, will affect everything. It will decide what will get you out of bed in the morning, what you will do with your evenings, how you will spend your weekends, what you read, who you know, what breaks your heart, and what amazes you with joy and gratitude. Fall in love, stay in love, and it will decide everything.

Many might disagree with Kathy's methods, and most are not called to her path of resistance as a way of life. But few would doubt the sincerity of her convictions. Where would we be without people like her to urge our consciences off the beaten track?

3

LOVE TENDERLY

There is a sort of lamentation and loving-kindness as well as a little wisdom somewhere inside me that cry to be let out.

—Etty Hillesum

To say that I am made in the image of God is to say that love is the reason for my existence, for God is love. Love is my true identity. Selflessness is my true self. Love is my true character. Love is my name.

—Thomas Merton

THERE ARE SEVERAL translations of Micah 6:8. The main difference is in how the *love* part gets translated. The Jerusalem Bible uses the phrase "to love tenderly," with the adverb *tenderly* highlighting a certain quality of kindness or gentleness toward the object of our love. The New Revised Standard Version uses a different phrase, "to love kindness." This translation is probably closer to the sense of the original Hebrew word used by Micah, *hesed,* a noun that has been variously translated as "kindness," "love," "mercy," "loving-kindness," "steadfast love," "loyalty," and "solidarity." In this sense we are being urged to love *love,* to make love itself the object of our affection and devotion, to let love govern our lives. As an old Quaker hymn puts it:

> Since love is Lord of heaven and earth,
>   how can I keep from singing?

This chapter is an exploration of love and vocation, centering on the idea that loving inclinations have their origins in certain tender movements of the heart. Loving feelings exercise a certain moral tug upon our hearts. I focus particularly on feelings of affection and compassion, by which we feel *for* others or *with* others. But love is not only a feeling. It is also a *choice* we make or action we take, regardless of the feeling of the moment. *Steadfast love* calls for tenacity and commitment over the long haul, even in trying times.

It is possible for us to experience loving feelings and make loving commitments in many dimensions of our lives, including our family life, our love life, our work, and through our engagement with people and issues in the wider world. By way of example, I look at two callings that require tremendous commitment and provision of a lot of tender loving care: the vocation of parenting and the calling to care for declining elders as they approach the end of their lives.

TENDER LOVING CARE

Affection is a tender feeling of fondness or liking that spontaneously wells up in our hearts as we regard persons who are dear to us. Such feelings toward loved ones give rise to all kinds of caring and protective inclinations that motivate us to attend to their needs and look out for their safety and well-being. No doubt there is a biological or instinctual basis for the affectionate ties that bind parents and children, couples, friends, families, and communities.

If it is true that God is love, and that human beings are made in the image of God, then there is also a way that we are *spiritually* wired for tenderness. In both the Hebrew and Christian scriptures there are numerous examples of God's capacity for affection and tender, loving care. Among other imagery (warrior, king, and so on), God is portrayed as an attentive mother, a kind father, a devoted spouse, a loyal sibling, and a true friend.

There are lovely examples from the book of Isaiah. In one passage God's devotion is likened to that of a nursing mother, ever attuned to and preoccupied with the needs of the infant who depends on her:

> Can a woman forget her nursing child,
>> or show no compassion for the child of her
>> womb?
> Even these may forget,
>> yet I will not forget you. (Is 49:15)

In another passage, best known from Handel's *Messiah*, God speaks in a tender, reassuring tone, like a parent soothing a distressed child:

> Comfort, O comfort my people,
>> says your God.
> Speak tenderly to Jerusalem
>> and cry to her. (Is 40:1–2)

And in another we are invited into a poignant, intimate conversation between God and Isaiah's mysterious servant figure, who is addressed by God in a way not unlike the promises couples make to each other on their wedding day:

> I have called you by name, you are mine. . . .
> Because you are precious in my sight,
>   and honored, and I love you. (Is 43:1, 4)

And, of course, there is Jesus, full to overflowing with tender love and compassion. Everything we know about him suggests that this love welled up from the depths of his unique sense of loving intimacy with God. Jesus addressed God as *abba*, an Aramaic word he seems to have used as a familiar term of endearment, something analogous to English words like *Dad* or *Papa*.[1] It is not important that he used a male term to refer to God. What matters is that he knew himself as a beloved child of God and that he experienced God as a warm, caring, affectionate parent. God was not a remote abstraction for Jesus, a theological idea that one "believes" in or not. God was his *abba,* a presence, an inner voice that whispered encouraging and loving things to him in the tone of a proud, supportive parent. All of this is evident in the voice Jesus is said to have heard during his baptism by John the Baptist at the Jordan River:

> And a voice came from heaven, "You are my Son, the Beloved; with you I am well pleased." (Mk 1:11; Lk 3:22)

The voice reveals something to Jesus about who *he* is, but it also reveals something important about who God is—and *how God feels*. Although the parallel passage in the Gospel of Matthew describes the voice as if it were addressed more generally to all present at the river ("*This* is my beloved Son . . . "), the Gospels of Mark and Luke suggest that it was addressed personally to Jesus ("*You* are my beloved Son . . . "), perhaps in the form of

---

[1] There are three uses of *abba* in the New Testament: Mark 14:36, Galatians 4:6, and Romans 8:15. Albert Nolan explores Jesus's use of the term in *Jesus before Christianity* (Maryknoll, NY: Orbis Books, 1976/2001) and also in *Jesus Today* (Maryknoll, NY: Orbis Books, 2006).

a powerful inner experience that Jesus later recalled and shared with his friends and disciples.

A central feature of Jesus's own calling was a passionate desire to put other people in touch with a similar experience of themselves as beloved sons and daughters of God: "As the Father has loved me, so I have loved you" (Jn 15:9) "The starting point of Jesus' spirituality," writes Albert Nolan, "the experience of God as *abba*, included the awareness that God was a loving Father to *all human beings*."[2] Knowing oneself as a beloved son or daughter of God makes it possible to regard an ever-widening and inclusive circle of people as brothers and sisters. It also inclines us to *treat* them as such. Children who are secure in the knowledge that they are loved are more capable of loving; people who have received empathy develop a deeper capacity for empathy with others. The First Letter of John eloquently lays out the spiritual dynamic:

> Beloved, let us love one another, because love is from God; everyone who loves is born of God and knows God. Whoever does not love does not know God, for God is love. . . . Beloved, since God loved us so much, we also ought to love one another. . . . Those who say, "I love God," and hate their brothers or sisters, are liars; for those who do not love a brother or sister whom they have seen, cannot love God whom they have not seen . . . those who love God must love their brothers and sisters also. (1 Jn 14:7–8, 11, 16, 19–21)

Descending from these exalted spiritual heights to the messy and complicated realities of the world and human relationships, we are all too aware that love is not easy. Many people are hard to love, and we ourselves may sometimes be hard to love. To one

---

[2] Nolan, *Jesus Today*, 79.

degree or another, all of us have doubts about whether we are loved or lovable. Allowing ourselves to love and be loved is risky; it makes us vulnerable to being hurt or disappointed or rejected. We both need and fear love; we crave it and resist it.

Although many were receptive to Jesus's radical message of unconditional love, we know that he ultimately met with rejection and violent hostility. In the Gospels there is a mounting sense of tension and suspense as Jesus approaches Jerusalem, knowing full well that confrontations with the religious and political authorities there were not likely to go well. Some poignant passages suggest that Jesus experienced a kind of tender, maternal feeling toward the people of Jerusalem, accompanied by a profound sense of disappointment and heartbreak that his loving overtures were going to be cruelly rebuffed:

> "Jerusalem, Jerusalem, the city that kills the prophets and stones those who are sent to it! How often have I desired to gather you together as a hen gathers her brood under her wings, and you were not willing!" (Lk 13:34)

> As he came near and saw the city, he wept over it, saying, "If you, even you, had only recognized on this day the things that make for peace! But now they are hidden from your eyes." (Lk 19:41)

When Jesus entered the city things quickly turned dark and ominous. He apparently became more confrontational and provocative by creating a disturbance at the Temple, which triggered such anxiety in the authorities that they began plotting to kill him. In short order he was arrested, publicly tortured, and executed by crucifixion. For Jesus, though, even this grim end became an occasion for more love, deeper love, greater love: "No one has greater love than this, to lay down one's life for one's friends" (Jn 15:13).

COMPASSION AND EMPATHY

Compassion is another tender movement of the heart.[3] Affection is a tender feeling *for* others; compassion is characterized by feeling *with* others. It is the feeling we experience when we are touched or moved by their pain or need. The Latin root of the word *compassion* means "to suffer with" or "together-suffering."

Compassionate feelings are always accompanied by merciful inclinations to relieve the suffering that has affected us. The Merriam-Webster dictionary defines *compassion* as "the sympathetic consciousness of others' distress together with a desire to alleviate it." The distress moves us on an inward emotional level, but we also feel moved to *do* something about it. This could include anything from hearing and responding the cry of the baby at 3 a.m. to hearing and responding to the "cry of the poor" in the wider world. In the first case, we are obviously called upon to get up to see whether the baby needs to be fed or changed or comforted. The more complex problem of poverty calls for conscientious discernment and consideration of how we may be personally called to respond to the problem of social suffering in the world. Many callings have their origins in such stirrings of the heart. Compassion, vocation, and conscience are related, because the right thing to do is usually the loving thing to do.

Compassion is related to *empathy,* which is a broader and more inclusive capacity to be affected not only by suffering but also by the whole range of human experience. Specifically, empathy is the conscious and intentional effort to feel or imagine ourselves in the world of others in order to know something of what they are experiencing at any given time. We might share a measure

---

[3] Some of this material on compassion is adapted from John Neafsey, "Passion and Compassion: The Heart's Calling," in *A Sacred Voice Is Calling: Personal Vocation and Social Conscience* (Maryknoll, NY: Orbis Books, 2006).

of sorrow for their pain or misfortune, but we might also feel positive feelings of joy or relief or pride over their personal achievements or good fortune.

In my clinical work with survivors of torture I have sometimes experienced what is known as vicarious trauma. This occurs when caregivers, through the process of empathy, find themselves experiencing thoughts and feelings that resemble those of the traumatized person for whom they are caring. But I have also shared in the joy and exhilarating sense of liberation that survivors experience over victories big and small. This includes everything from the blessed relief of getting a good night's sleep after years of insomnia and nightmares to the profound sense of validation and gratitude they experience when they are finally granted political asylum in the United States.

I once had the pleasure of working closely with a fine person who had endured unspeakable torture in his homeland, after which he suffered for years from severe post-traumatic stress and depression. On the day he was finally granted asylum by the immigration court, I have a fond memory of sharing a celebratory drink with him and his friends at a restaurant near the courthouse. Toasts and prayers of thanksgiving were offered for this small, precious, personal victory for justice, and for the opportunity it offered to begin the challenging process of building a new life for himself in a new place.

The ability to listen empathically to another person, and then to communicate our empathic understanding in such a way that he or she feels understood, is the basis of all genuine connection and understanding between human beings. Empathy is a crucial component of the healing process of psychotherapy. The "talking cure" originally developed by Sigmund Freud is now associated with a diverse range of theoretical principles and therapeutic techniques, but none of them is effective unless it is grounded in empathic connection and understanding. In an unguarded moment Freud once wrote in a letter to Jung: "Essentially, one might say the cure is effected through love."[4]

There are limits to our capacity to appreciate fully and to understand the world of other persons. This is especially the case with those who are significantly different from us in one way or another in terms of race, class, culture, religion, gender, sexual orientation, politics, or any other important feature of personal experience or identity. Nonetheless, our sense of common humanity, empathic feelings, and imagination offer potentials for understanding and connection across these divides of difference.

Empathy does not always come easily, and it is harder to empathize with some people than others. It can sometimes be difficult to connect with people who have been deeply hurt or traumatized, in some cases because they have developed complex defense mechanisms to help them avoid feeling their own pain and to keep others at a safe emotional distance. It may also take considerable patience and effort to develop empathy with people who have anger problems that make them hard to like or feel close to.

People in strained, conflictual relationships face special challenges in learning to listen with empathy and to understand each other. These emotional and relational dynamics also apply beyond the one-to-one interpersonal situation to collective relationships among communities and nations, especially when there has been a history of hurt and suspicion and hostility. Jesus urged us to love our enemies, but I don't think he meant we have to *like* those whom we oppose. I am quite sure, though, that he meant we should at least try to *respect* and *understand* them. In *Crucified People* I explore some of the challenges of healing, forgiveness,

---

[4] Sigmund Freud to C. G. Jung, letter, December 6, 1906, in *The Freud/Jung Letters,* ed. William McGuire (Princeton, NJ: Princeton University Press, 1994 <1974>).

and reconciliation in nations with histories of massive historical trauma.[5]

Empathy and compassion are integral to our sense of social conscience. An uneasy conscience prompts us to think seriously about social suffering that has come to our attention. This makes it possible for us to recognize ways that unjust conditions, policies, attitudes, and ideologies hurt and deprive particular people in particular ways. Compassionate feelings in response to "noticed pain" have the potential to unsettle the comfortable status quo of our lives. They exercise a certain moral tug upon our hearts and pull us toward merciful and just action. The opposite of compassion is *indifference,* a sense of numbness and apathy and complacency about, for example, the plight of the poor and the oppressed. "The replacing of numbness with compassion," writes Brueggemann, "that is, the end of cynical indifference and the beginning of noticed pain, signals a social revolution."[6]

Because of our unique personal backgrounds and histories, our hearts may be particularly responsive to certain kinds of people or problems. Universal compassion for all humanity is a worthy ideal, but on a practical level most of us are more likely to identify with the sufferings or aspirations of particular groups of people. Some people's hearts might be particularly responsive to children with special needs, while others might feel drawn to care for refugees, or oppressed minorities, or women subject to domestic violence. Sometimes very specific vocations grow out of a feeling of "suffering with" certain kinds of people.

Gospel accounts suggest that Jesus had a remarkably deep and broad capacity for compassion for a wide range of people in his society who were excluded and marginalized by poverty,

---

[5] See John Neafsey, "Healing of the Nations: Guilt, Sorrow, and Forgiveness," in *Crucified People.*

[6] Walter Brueggemann, *The Prophetic Imagination* (Minneapolis, MN: Fortress Press, 2001), 91.

illness, or social shame and disgrace. Albert Nolan provides a comprehensive list:

> The people to whom Jesus turned his attention are referred to in the gospels by a variety of terms: the poor, the blind, the lame, the crippled, the lepers, the hungry, the miserable (those who weep), sinners, prostitutes, tax collectors, demoniacs (those possessed by unclean spirits), the persecuted, the downtrodden, the captives, all who labor and are overburdened, the rabble who know nothing of the law, the crowds, the little ones, the least, the last and the babes and the lost sheep of the house of Israel.[7]

The Greek word for compassion in the New Testament is *splagchnizomai*, which means "to be moved in the inward parts."[8] It is suggestive of a deep, heartfelt feeling or gut reaction to suffering. Many passages specifically mention Jesus's inner response to people. He was "moved with pity" (NRSV) or "moved with compassion" (KJV) for a leper (Mk 1:41). "When he saw the crowds, he had compassion for them, because they were harassed and helpless, like sheep without a shepherd" (Mt 9:36). In one of Jesus's most well-known parables, what distinguished the Samaritan, that is, what *made* him good, was his compassionate response to the man who had been left half-dead by robbers (Lk 10:25–37).

There is a mysterious way that compassion and empathy can put us in touch with the heart of God. Along these lines, Abraham Joshua Heschel wrote of the *pathos* of God, the divine capacity to be personally moved and inwardly affected by what is happening in the world: "The reaction of the divine self, its manifestation in the form of love, mercy, disappointment, or

---

[7] Nolan, *Jesus before Christianity*, 27.
[8] See ibid., 35. See also Brueggemann, *The Prophetic Imagination,* 89.

anger convey the profound intensity of the divine inwardness."[9]
We see evidence of this divine pathos or empathy in the Book
of Exodus:

> "I have observed the misery of my people who are in
> Egypt; I have heard their cry on account of their taskmas-
> ters. Indeed, I know their sufferings." (Ex 3:7)

Through empathy, God *knows* the misery and suffering of the
people under slavery and oppression. It has been observed, heard,
felt, known. Similarly, in another passage the people are encouraged to remember their own history, to recall what it *felt* like
to be oppressed, so that they will not oppress or mistreat others:

> You shall not oppress a stranger, for you know the heart of
> a stranger, because you were strangers in the land of Egypt.
> (Ex 23:9, NKJV)

Paradoxically, there is a way that personal experiences of
suffering can make us sensitive to the suffering of others. The
memory of our own pain, even if our personal experience is
not identical or equivalent, enables us to empathize and identify
with the "stranger." We were once strangers ourselves, and so we
know what it feels like to be a stranger.

STEADFAST LOVE

The Hebrew word *hesed* has several rich meanings and connotations. One of these is "steadfast love," which is characterized by
a kind of tenacity or fierceness in our loving commitments over
the long haul, even in trying times. The Book of Hosea offers

---

[9] Abraham Joshua Heschel, *The Prophets* (New York: Harper Perennial,
1962), 29.

a rich and complex example. Hosea lived roughly around the time of Micah during the eighth century BCE. We know little about him other than the peculiar story he tells of his troubled marriage to a woman named Gomer, which is at the heart of his short book. Gomer apparently had a checkered past; she may have been involved in prostitution or other relationships that gave her a certain reputation. The greater part of the book is an account of Hosea's efforts to grapple with his dark feelings of hurt and shame and anger about his wife's history and character. His testimony reveals an intense, passionate soul capable of both great anger and great love, which are in constant tension throughout the book. Through his personal anguish, Hosea learned some deep and fundamental lessons about himself, the nature of God, and the resilience and redemptive power of love.

Scholars disagree on whether the marriage story is actually autobiographical. But there is no doubt that Hosea meant the story to be an allegory for the strained relationship between God and Israel, drawing a stark contrast between divine faithfulness and human idolatry and betrayal. Throughout, Hosea alternates between the voice of the husband pained about his marriage and the voice of the prophet who is pained about the state of the nation. Rabbi Heschel, who believed there must have been some historical basis for Hosea's unusual story, suggests that the prophet's marital troubles were likely the very thing that enabled him to attain such a depth of empathy and emotional solidarity with God:

> As time went by, Hosea became aware of the fact that his personal fate was a mirror of the divine pathos, that his sorrow echoed the sorrow of God. . . . Only by living through in his own life what the divine Consort of Israel experienced, was the prophet able to attain sympathy for the divine situation.[10]

---

[10] Heschel, *The Prophets,* 69.

The story begins with Hosea being directed by God to marry Gomer, who is variously described with considerable derision as a prostitute or adulteress:

> When the Lord first spoke through Hosea, the Lord said to Hosea, "Go, take for yourself a wife of whoredom and have children of whoredom, for the land commits great whoredom by forsaking the Lord." (Hos 1:2)

> The Lord said to me again, "Go, love a woman who has a lover and is an adulteress, just as the Lord loves the people of Israel, though they turn to other gods and love raisin cakes." (Hos 3:1)

Hosea's language is problematic and off-putting because of its blatant sexism. There is certainly a timeless, lyrical power to many of Hosea's oracles, but it is evident that in some ways he was also a man of his patriarchal times.[11] With this in mind, if we are able to suspend judgment about some of Hosea's culture-bound imagery, some important lessons about redemptive potentials for reconciliation and working things out in more equitable relationships can be discerned.

From the beginning it is obvious that the figure of Gomer is a metaphor for the nation of Israel. Her history of infidelity and promiscuity is equated with the people's *idolatry*, their turning away from the true God toward lesser gods, false gods—everything from superficial pleasure ("raisin cakes") to the worship of Baal (one of the local Canaanite deities). Hosea and Gomer

---

[11] For a thoughtful feminist analysis of prophetic language and imagery, including Hosea's use of the marriage metaphor in the ancient patriarchal context, see Julia M. O'Brien, *Challenging Prophetic Metaphors: Theology and Ideology in the Prophets* (Louisville, KY: Westminster John Knox, 2008). See also Daniel Berrigan's fascinating, highly political meditations on Hosea in *Minor Prophets, Major Themes* (Marion, SD: Fortkamp Publishing/Rose Hill Books, 1995).

have children, each of whom is given a symbolic name suggestive of profound alienation, rejection, and estrangement (a daughter, for example, is named Lo-ruhamah, which means "not pitied," and a son is named Lo-ammi, "not my people"). Later chapters detail how Hosea wrestles with his dark inclinations to punish or give up on Gomer, which is mirrored by how God is feeling in relation to Israel.

In ancient patriarchal cultures, and even in some places in the world today, real or imagined sins on the part of a woman can be a life-or-death matter for her. Think of the New Testament story about the woman caught in adultery, in which Jesus confronts the outraged, self-righteous mob of men who are about to stone her to death. "Let anyone among you who is without sin," he says, "be the first to throw a stone at her" (Jn 8:7). In this case a humbling self-awareness of moral imperfection acted as a restraining factor against violent acting out. They dropped the stones.

Eventually, there is a poignant reconciliation and re-betrothal between Hosea and Gomer and, by analogy, between God and Israel. In spite of everything, love wins out. Hosea does not give up on Gomer, and God does not give up on the people. The moral of the story, of course, is that we should not give up on one another. Steadfast love calls for a kind of persistence and determination to see if it is possible to work things out. This applies to all kinds of personal relationships (couples, parents and children, friends, neighbors, co-workers, and more) as well as to larger relational dynamics within and among communities and nations. It can also apply to our relationship with *ourselves* in all our various individual and collective identities. Is it possible to recover a sense of integrity and authenticity even when we have been untrue to who we really are?

Hosea's story can be taken on a social and political level, which is clearly one of the ways he meant for it to be understood. The prophet was in grief over the state of the nation.

Israel had betrayed its founding covenant and ideals, lost its soul, forsaken the God of love and justice.

> Hear the word of the Lord, O people of Israel;
>   for the Lord has an indictment against the
>   inhabitants of the land.
> There is no faithfulness or loyalty,
>   and no knowledge of God in the land. (Hos
>   4:1)

When a national or institutional culture strays from its founding ideals and principles, people sometimes experience a kind of countercultural call to preserve or recover a sense of integrity and authenticity. For some years my parish community at the Church of Saint Gertrude in Chicago has claimed the motto *All Are Welcome.* This was initially meant to serve as a friendly signal to gay and lesbian Catholics, especially those who might be unsure about how they might be received by an institution with a history of considerable homophobia and intolerance. In recent months the welcome has become more inclusive. The parish, in partnership with the local Catholic Charities refugee resettlement office, has decided to sponsor a refugee family from Syria. We hope to make it possible for a family that has had to flee danger and persecution to get a new start in a safe place. In a national climate of fear and hostility toward immigrants and refugees, it is a chance for our community to live up to our motto: *All Are Welcome.* For us, *all* includes men, women, and children from Syria—whether they are Christian or Muslim.

Hosea's story also can apply on a personal level. There is a sense of disappointment and disillusionment in Hosea as he attempts to come to terms with the imperfect human reality of his partner. All of us can resonate with this in some way, beginning with our relationships with all the various imperfect people in our lives who may not always be easy to love. This goes both ways, of course, since they must also deal with *us* in all our imperfection. Couples often struggle with such feelings, especially after the honeymoon phase of being "in love" wears off and they begin to face the challenging day-to-day reality of keeping their love alive over the long haul. If there is a serious conflict or, worse, a betrayal that undermines basic trust, things become especially challenging. The question then is whether it is possible to recover trust and good will toward each other at all. There are no easy answers! Each partner must consult his or her own heart to discern whether reconciliation is possible in this particular situation. Sometimes it is not.

When people feel mistreated or betrayed, they may be inclined to strike back in retaliatory anger to punish the one who has disrespected or hurt them. A good part of the Book of Hosea documents the struggles of the prophet (and God) with feelings of anger and rage. "It is the dark side of love outraged, of hope contemned," writes Berrigan.[12] It is clear that Hosea is feeling hurt, petulant, contemptuous, punitive, vindictive—and he is tempted to take it out on Gomer and the children:

> Upon her children also I will have no pity,
>   because they are children of whoredom.
>   (Hos 2:4)

In a parallel spiritual universe, God is in a punitive mood toward the people of Israel. God and Hosea wrestle with these raw feelings throughout the book, and at some points there is considerable suspense as to whether things will work out at all. If we are honest, we will recognize ourselves in all of this; the reactions of Hosea and God reveal our own shadow side.

---

[12] Berrigan, *Minor Prophets, Major Themes,* 69.

The challenge in emotionally charged situations and relationships is to cultivate an attitude of *conscious, loving self-restraint*.[13]
The "conscious" part has to do with honestly acknowledging
our feelings of hurt and anger (at least to ourselves), along with
all the accompanying unloving inclinations we might feel to
withdraw or retaliate in some way. Then comes the "loving self-
restraint." In the interest of integrity, and to preserve and protect
the future of a valued relationship with someone we love, it is
necessary to contain or modulate or restrain our inclinations to
act on our feelings. We choose *not* to say the things we feel like
saying, to do the things we feel like doing. In the heat of the moment, when we are tempted to say or do something hurtful, we
try to remember the bigger picture and think better of it. This
does not mean we should not be assertive or expressive when
these reactions are called for. The problem lies in the temptation
to be aggressive or destructive. Self-restraint in the interest of the
greater good is the foundation of everything from personal tact
to international diplomacy to Gandhian nonviolence.

Hosea learns conscious, loving self-restraint. His anger toward
Gomer subsides. He has pity on the daughter he had cruelly
named Not Pitied. He finds it within himself to say, "You are
my people," to the son he had named Not My People (Hos
2:23). He recovers an affectionate connection with Gomer and
the children.

> My heart recoils within me;
>   my compassion grows warm and tender.
> I will not execute my fierce anger. (Hos 11:8–9)

---

[13] This phrase comes from John Maltsberger and Dan Buie, who write
about troubled people who provoke strong emotional reactions in the profes-
sionals who care for them. See J. T. Maltsberger and D. H. Buie, "Counter-
transference Hate in the Treatment of Suicidal Patients," *Archives of General
Psychiatry* 30/5 (May 1974): 625–33.

God also chooses to try again with Israel:

> I will heal their disloyalty;
>> I will love them freely,
>> for my anger has turned from them. (Hos
>> 14:4)

Hosea resolves to court Gomer once again, and he renews his promise to love her:

> Therefore, I will now allure her,
>> and bring her into the wilderness,
>> and speak tenderly to her. . . .

> And I will take you for my wife forever; I will take you for my wife in righteousness and in justice, in steadfast love, and in mercy. (Hos 2:14, 19)

Through his troubles Hosea learned something very important about the difference between the feeling of the moment and the promise of always and forever. "Over and above the immediate and contingent emotional reaction of the Lord," writes Heschel, "we are informed about the eternal and basic disposition."[14] Perhaps Hosea also learned to differentiate his own emotional reactions from God's reactions. He was not God, and neither are we. And yet it is always humanly possible for us to make a conscious, intentional choice to start over, to try again, to love and be loved again—no matter what. By doing so, we align our imperfect, finite selves as best we can with the divine, eternal disposition: steadfast love.

---

[14] Heschel, *The Prophets*, 59.

PARENTHOOD

One recent Saturday night my family (me; my wife, Maura; our twelve-year-old daughter, Rosie; and our fifteen-year-old son, Bryan) gathered in the living room to watch the movie *Parenthood*. I had expected a light comedy involving the chaotic and rather crazy extended family featured in the movie. Instead, I found myself stunned by the depth of emotional pain and strain and grief in many members of this fictional family. These include an anxious little boy needing to go for his first visit to the psychiatrist, a couple struggling with serious marital problems, a divorced mother worried about her teenage daughter's too-early ventures into sex and love, a depressed and angry adolescent boy who feels abandoned by his father, an uncle with a severe addiction, a husband whose work and family life are tremendously out of balance, and more. Thankfully, there was a little comedic relief and, in spite of it all, some heartening evidence of resilience and redemptive love.

The vocation of parenthood is not for the faint of heart. Our character and our capacity for steadfast love can be sorely tested in the crucible of the family experience. Under the press of constant demands to keep the ship afloat, good feeling can dissipate and be replaced by emotional depletion and irritability. The good intentions of parents can be undermined by unresolved issues from their own childhoods that are triggered by the emotional demands of caring for children. Parenting can potentially bring out the best in us but, if we are honest, we know it can occasionally bring out the worst. Sometimes we "lose it," and apologies are in order.

All this being said, we still experience a deep, instinctual need to be generative, to bring new life into the world, to be fruitful and multiply, to play our own part in the drama of creation. Many do this literally by starting their own families and raising children. But there are many other ways to be generative besides bringing children into the world. I know many profoundly generative people who, for various reasons, do not have biological children of their own, but who nonetheless have brought all kinds of wonderful new life into the world through their creative work and loving service. Others have found their calling by providing homes for foster and adopted children who need a safe, nurturing place to grow up.

More basic even than the quality of parental interaction with children is the crucial vocation of simply *providing*. Think of the exhausting lives of many parents who work inconvenient hours at unsatisfying jobs in order to pay the rent and meet the basic survival needs of their families, or of immigrants who work at low-paying jobs but nonetheless manage to wire a staggering percentage of their meager wages back to impoverished loved ones in their home countries.

It can help to think of parenting as a spiritual practice, as in the apt title of a thoughtful book by Bonnie Miller-McLemore: *In the Midst of Chaos: Parenting as Spiritual Practice.* "I want to redeem the chaos of care as a site of God's good news," writes Miller-McLemore. "What would happen . . . if we were to search for spiritual wisdom by looking closely at messy, familial ways of living?"[15] The aim of such a perspective on parenting is not just to bring order out of chaos, or for parents to learn to say and do all the right things so that children can be perfectly formed into the kind of individuals we want them to be. The spirituality of parenting is not just about formation of children; it is also about the self-discovery and transformation of the adults who care for them.

Parenting as a spiritual practice requires tremendous inner work, especially in the area of mindful self-awareness and psychological honesty with ourselves. Myla and Jon Kabat-Zinn

---

[15] Bonnie Miller-McLemore, *In the Midst of Chaos: Parenting as Spiritual Practice* (San Francisco, CA: John Wiley and Sons, 2007), xiv.

have written a beautiful book that applies the wisdom of the mindfulness meditation tradition to the care of children: *Everyday Blessings: The Inner Work of Mindful Parenting.*[16] Mindfulness meditation is an ancient Buddhist practice of cultivating compassionate, non-judgmental self-awareness of whatever we happen to be experiencing at any given moment. There is a way that such mindfulness can help us to move from a harried experience of family life as "one damn thing after another" to a sense of gratitude and appreciation for the blessing of the present moment—even in the midst of stress and apparent chaos.

Conscious, loving self-restraint is certainly a crucial component of mindful parenting, because children tend to stir up all kinds of intense emotional reactions in the adults who care for them. Careful reflection on such feelings can teach us a great deal about ourselves. This is especially the case in the parenting of children with special needs, as I learned again and again in my work at clinics for children and families caught up in the Child Protective Services system. Because all of the children had backgrounds of severe abuse or neglect in their families of origin, many were living with foster parents or relatives. Some of the most wounded kids had developed attachment problems that made it hard for them to trust or connect with others in healthy ways, including some of the well-intentioned caregivers who were trying to provide loving homes for them.

Sadly, some kids seemed to have a way of unconsciously getting otherwise kind and capable caregivers to feel so upset that they were at risk of becoming abusive or of feeling so defeated that they might even be tempted to give up on the child. It is as if some children are compelled to repeat or reenact their past trauma of abuse or neglect in their present situation. There are situations in which the most important way to help these kids

---

[16] Myla and Jon Kabat-Zinn, *Everyday Blessings: The Inner Work of Mindful Parenting* (New York: Hachette Books, 1997).

is to provide emotional and moral support to the beleaguered adults in their lives, which includes helping them to practice conscious, loving self-restraint. This is much easier said than done, especially in the heat of the moment.

My wife, Maura, and I found our particular path to parenthood through international adoption. We met, fell very much in love, and began our married life together thinking that the next natural step would be to share the joys and responsibilities of parenting together. We assumed that children would come along in good time. But, like many couples, after years of trying and disappointment after disappointment, we discovered that infertility would make it impossible for us to have biological children; For a time we were quite demoralized and numb with grief.

Eventually, inspired by the example of some other couples from our community, we began to consider the option of adoption. This required getting used to the idea that our generativity and care could be expressed in a different way than we had imagined. Because of Maura's fluency in Spanish and her connections with Latin America and the Latino community through her work, we explored the possibility of international adoption from Guatemala. There were many scary unknowns inherent in such a process, as well as daunting logistical and financial costs. But I remember quite distinctly the moment when I said to Maura, with great conviction, "If we are going to go broke, we might as well make it a spiritual adventure! Let's do it." In short order we were off to Guatemala City to meet a darling infant boy, Bryan Antonio, who was to become our son. A couple of years later we returned to meet a lovely baby girl, Rosa Francesca, who was to become our daughter.

Through this process we became quite familiar with the territory of what is known in adoption circles as the "triad of grief," which refers to the various losses that are experienced by the birth mother, the adopted child, and the adoptive parents. First of all, there is the grief of the birth mother, who, because of her circumstances, feels that she must make a decision to relinquish care of her child. Then there is the grief of the adopted child, who, even if adopted as an infant, is always aware on some level of this profound loss at the beginning of his or her life. Finally, there is the grief of the adoptive parents, whose decision to adopt has often emerged out of their own grief.[17]

And yet, out of this grief all around, and through the mysteries of fate and destiny, a new family is born. We sometimes sang the song "Happy Adoption Day" to the children at bedtime:

> Oh, who would have guessed, who could have
>   seen
> Who could have possibly known
> All these roads we have traveled, the places
>   we've been
> Would have finally taken us home?
>
> There are those who think families happen by
>   chance
> A mystery their whole life through
> But we had a voice and we had a choice
> We were working and waiting for you.
>
> No matter the name and no matter the age
> No matter how you came to be
> No matter the skin, we are all of us kin
> We are all of us one family.
>
> So its here's to you, and three cheers to you
> Let's shout it, "Hip, hip, hip, hooray!"
> For, out of a world so tattered and torn,

---

[17] See Deborah N. Silverstein and Sharon Kaplan, "Lifelong Issues in Adoption," on the http://www.americanadoptioncongress.org website.

> You came to our house on that wonderful
> morn
> And all of a sudden this family was born
> Oh, happy adoption day![18]

Adoptive families, like all families, can be complicated. Among other things, one obvious issue is the scenario in which children and parents come from different racial backgrounds—in our case, when fair-skinned parents of Irish descent have children who are the lovely shade of brown of the indigenous Mayan people of Central America. When Bryan was little, he once commented on this difference: "Mommy and Daddy are Irish, but me and Rosie are Guatemalish." When he was ten years old, we took a short trip together to Guatemala, including a visit to an area where people speak one of the Mayan languages of his ancestors. When we returned to Chicago, he talked about how it was good to be home, but also about how Guatemala was *also* his home and how this made him feel "torn inside."

My daughter Rosie's heritage has made it easier for her to identify with the Native American experience. One memorable day when she was about seven years old, I happened to be reading a book about the defeat of General Custer at the hands of the Lakota Sioux warriors at the famous battle often referred to as Custer's Last Stand. Rosie was curious and asked what the book was about; I explained in terms I thought a child her age could understand. It was necessary to state the fact that the mission of Custer's white soldiers was to facilitate the theft of ancestral lands that rightfully belonged to the Native Americans.

It turned out that I underestimated Rosie's ability to "get" the story. Without missing a beat she put the whole thing together

---

[18] "Happy Adoption Day" can be heard on the John McCutcheon album *Family Garden* on Rounder Records. Lyrics by John McCutcheon (©1992, J. McCutcheon/Appalsongs).

in very personal terms: "*Your* team lost?" I nodded, a little taken
aback that I had been automatically assigned to Custer's "white"
team. She followed with another question: "*My* team won?"
I nodded again. Then, with a mischievous smile, she laughed:
"Ha, Ha!" I felt moved and proud that my spirited daughter was
already beginning to develop a consciousness of who she was,
where she came from, and how things usually go for the poor
and the different. And that, every once in a while, against all
odds, the tables are completely turned. The Magnificat or "Song
of Mary" comes to mind:

> He has brought down the powerful from their
>   thrones,
>   and lifted up the lowly.
> He has filled the hungry with good things,
>   and sent the rich away empty. (Lk 1:52–53)

All families are a microcosm of the world at large, in which
we are called to act justly, love tenderly, and walk humbly with
God. But the best way to teach children how to act "out there"
is to model justice, kindness, and humility in how we treat one
another in our day-to-day life at home. "We fail to recognize
the family as the heart and soul of doing justice," says Miller-
McLemore. "It is the place where justice is first learned and
practiced, and the place where we might begin to turn the world
upside down."[19]

In family life, justice is embodied through equitably sharing
what we have and treating one another fairly in matters big and
small. It can also take the form of "tough love," that is, holding
one another accountable, with fair and fitting consequences
for misbehavior. Practicing justice enters into everything from
taking turns at games to the management of negotiations about

---

[19] Miller-McLemore, *In the Midst of Chaos,* 103.

which television program to watch next. Kindness is practiced in everything from basic courtesy to noticing when a family member is upset or hurting. Humility is practiced by everyone, including parents, especially when it is necessary to admit that we have made a mistake, by making apologies when they are due and by seeking forgiveness when it is needed. It is all good.

GRANDPA'S ROOM

One of the ways calls are extended to us is through the needs of our loved ones, including the elders in our lives. Their needs speak to us and call for a response. As elders begin to decline, especially in advanced age, family members first experience inklings of such callings through an increased sense of concern and preoccupation with their well-being and safety. As their needs for care and supervision increase, we are challenged to consider our responsibilities to them, including the limits and boundaries of what we are *able* to do for them in any given circumstance. We must discern how we are called to care for them.

Over the last decade Maura and I witnessed the dramatic decline of both sets of our aging parents. Her mother, Josephine "Jo" Geissler, died at age eighty-five in December 2007; my mother, Louise Neafsey, died at age ninety in January 2010; and my father, Ed Neafsey, died at age ninety-seven in August 2011. Maura's father, Gene Geissler, the last of these four great elders, passed away at age ninety-nine in August 2012. All had lived long, rich lives, and all were able to die surrounded by loving family in their own homes or, in the case of my dad, in *my* home.

Because of the great longevity of our elders, each of our families became familiar with the rugged territory of advanced age: decreased energy and mobility, forgetfulness, risk of falling, and ever-increasing needs for closer supervision and care. Thankfully, both sets of parents were blessed with financial resources and plenty of supportive family. This made it possible for them to remain in their own homes—which they loved and hoped never to have to leave. Maura's sister Molly moved in with her parents to be a supportive presence in their later years. We were able to arrange for in-home care for my mom and dad to help with things like cooking, shopping, cleaning, bathing, trips to the doctor, and remembering to take medications at the proper times.

There was always a certain suspense that a serious mishap or fall might force the issue of a move to an assisted living or skilled-care facility. Living only five minutes from my parents' home, for years I made numerous emergency trips at odd times to assess the damage after Mom took a fall. Usually, she was able to pick herself up and dust herself off, but a few times we had to call the paramedics. A couple of months before her own death, Maura's mother took a catastrophic fall that turned out to be the beginning of the end. After amputation of her leg and a long hospital stay, Jo made it home just in time to be able to die in a hospital bed in her own living room, with her beloved husband, Gene, tenderly holding her hand. Five years later Gene died a similar blessed death in the same room.

My mom also died at home, with the merciful help of hospice care, with my dad at her side. After Mom was gone, Dad was suddenly alone, at age ninety-five, in the old house in which they had lived together for fifty years. He was a remarkably resilient man who masked his feelings well, but it was obvious that he was very lonely and very sad. Dad had been declining in a number of ways before Mom passed away, but the responsibility of seeing to her needs had always helped to keep him active and functioning and focused. Without his beloved life partner, though, he became listless and weak, was sometimes quite confused, and seemed increasingly unsteady on his feet. Even with round-the-clock in-home care, things were worrisome.

My sister Judy, my brothers E.J. and Jim, and I were discussing the possibility of arranging for Dad to move to a senior residential program. In the midst of these considerations, my wife, Maura, suggested that maybe we should consider the idea of having Dad come to live with us in *our* home. I found myself excited by the idea. It stayed with me, and we began to think about it more concretely. Dad could stay in our first-floor bedroom, so he wouldn't have to deal with stairs. The in-home caregivers could help us to take care of him. As with the earlier decision about international adoption, there was an unusual sense of peace and clarity about the inclination to care for Dad in our home. It felt like a *calling*.

The idea, of course, needed to be discussed with my siblings to confirm that they were in agreement that this was a prudent plan. With their unanimous consent, along with some concern about the potential for my own family to become overextended, we moved forward. A few elder-friendly safety renovations (safety bars, bed railings, and so on) needed attention. Ed Neafsey moved into our home on May 27, 2010, the occasion of his ninety-sixth birthday.

It was arranged that Dad's familiar caregivers would now come to our house seven days a week to allow my family to continue our regular daily activities. For all intents and purposes, two of these women became part of our family. They had a way of anticipating Dad's every need and had a deep appreciation for the importance of predictable routines in the lives of elderly persons. They also had a way of "going with the flow" that preserved and protected my dad's dignity. For example, because of the steady progress of his dementia, he would sometimes become befuddled and lost in the middle of a conversation, or even in mid sentence. This could be embarrassing for him. On one such occasion, one of his caregivers discreetly whispered to me, "Don't worry. I speak dementia." She meant that she was prepared to wait kindly and patiently for him to retrieve his original thought or, if this didn't work out, simply to move on to whatever happened to come next. The important thing was not to make him feel ashamed or self-conscious in any way.

Every day Dad and I would have a glass of wine together before dinner. This became our favorite daily ritual. I would entice him to get up from his long afternoon nap with the promise of the wine. Because he tended to be quite precarious on his feet, we would fill a wine glass with a mix of one-third white wine, one-third white grape juice, and one-third water. He really enjoyed it.

On pleasant days over the first summer he was with us, Dad and I enjoyed our wine in the shade of the back porch. Because of his dementia, and because he had always been a rather shy and reserved person, we did not talk every minute. Sometimes we just sat together. We happen to live in an area of Chicago that is below the flight path of planes that come in over Lake Michigan on their slow descent toward O'Hare airport, and so sometimes we just watched the slow procession of planes going over every couple of minutes. Dad sometimes seem surprised, and even a bit awestruck, when the next plane would come along: "Oh, look, there's another one!"

Afternoons with Dad forced me to slow down, to tune in to a different rhythm, to watch things unfold from the perspective of one present moment to the next. With him, I seemed to experience an altered sense of time and to enter into a kind of altered state of consciousness. I so looked forward to this time with him every day. Joyce Mercer writes beautifully of how older adults with dementia offer "time-gifts" to people who need to slow down:

> When I visit older adults, I experience the gift of time. It so profoundly reshapes my life that I have come to think of the vocation of the older adults (especially those with Alzheimer's and other forms of dementia) as offering time-gifts to people who need to slow down. In this way the callings of the ones receiving care are inextricably linked to the callings of the ones giving care. This dialectic is

central in the vocation of older adulthood, where receiving becomes the more visible element in daily life, but where giving takes place in unobserved ways.[20]

Although his dementia was becoming severe, every now and then Dad and I would have a memorable conversation as we sat together. Sometimes he was very lucid. For example, some dear friends lost their young son in a tragic drowning incident while Dad was with us, and he was very sympathetic and concerned about how they were doing. Also, at times it seemed that his dementia did not affect his long-term memory in quite the same way. One afternoon, out of the blue, he recalled and shared some poignant early memories of his own father, my grandfather, an Irish immigrant who died tragically when Dad was only seven— almost ninety years before. Dad was recalling very specific things he had probably heard people say at his father's wake, as if it had happened yesterday. As he reminisced, he even took on the accent of the Irish immigrants who had gathered to mourn the death of a young immigrant father.

It was good for the children to be around Grandpa, and it was good for him to be around them. The first-floor bedroom became Grandpa's room. The kids learned to watch the noise level, especially when Grandpa was sleeping (which was sometimes as much as sixteen hours a day) and to not make fast moves when he was making his way around the house with his walker. Even the pets tuned in to the need to be gentle around an elder; Ginny, our Australian cattle dog, seemed to know intuitively that she should be careful not to get underfoot.

Over the fifteen months Dad was with us, he continued to decline. It became necessary to build a ramp so that he could get

[20] Joyce Ann Mercer, "Older Adulthood: Vocation at Life's End," in *Calling All Years Good: Vocation across the Lifespan,* ed. Kathleen A. Cahalan and Bonnie J. Miller-McLemore (Grand Rapids, MI: Eerdmans, 2016).

out to the car for occasional medical appointments. It became harder and harder for him to get around, and eventually he couldn't even manage to get out to the porch for his afternoon glass of wine. We changed the venue to his room, so that he would just have to move a few feet across the floor from the bed to his chair. He sometimes became terribly exasperated at being so weak and old; at one point he cried out, "I can't *do* anything!" It felt humiliating to him. Seeing him like this also induced a humbling awareness of my own mortality and the prospect of my own eventual decline.

In August 2011, a few months after turning ninety-seven, Dad took a bad fall that necessitated a trip to the hospital. He hated the hospital, and we made the decision to start hospice care when he returned home so that he wouldn't have to make any more exhausting, disorienting trips out of the house. We arranged to replace his regular bed with a hospital bed. A few days later, when the ambulance crew wheeled his gurney up the ramp into our home for the last time, he was beaming. He was glad to be home.

Within a day it became clear that Dad was too weak to get out of bed; it turned out that he would never get out of bed again. After another few days he stopped eating, and the hospice nurse helped me to accept that he was preparing to die. That night, when he was still fairly lucid, I had a good talk with him. I leaned over him, held his hand, and looked into his eyes: "Dad, I think I should call E.J, Jim, and Judy, because it looks as though you are getting ready to make your final passage." He closed his eyes and clutched my hand. After I made the calls to my sister and brothers, I asked Dad if he might like a little taste of wine. He nodded. I gave a little to him in a medicine dropper; he swallowed and sighed and smiled. E.J. and Judy came over that evening, and Jim made it in from California the next day.

The next few days Dad began to slip in and out of consciousness, and then he started to slip away. Sometimes he seemed to be in an in-between place, somewhere between this world and the next. With his eyes closed, he would talk quietly to people who were not in the room; once he opened his eyes with a far-off look and a sweet smile, as if he was seeing something very beautiful.

The night he died there was a lovely stream of visitors who came by for a last little visit with Ed. He made his final passage around midnight. We decided to let his body stay with us over-night. Later that night, after the hospice nurse left, the family gathered by Dad's bedside and drank Bailey's Irish Cream from the Waterford crystal glasses that had been a gift from Dad's older sister.

We still refer to the first floor bedroom as Grandpa's room.

4

WALK HUMBLY

For all who exalt themselves will be humbled, and those who humble themselves will be exalted.

—Luke 14:11

The virtue called humility is deep-rooted in the deity.

—Meister Eckhart

MICAH USES THE Hebrew word *tsana*, meaning "humble" or "humbly," to convey the manner in which we are meant to walk or carry ourselves in the world. The Latin root of the English word *humility* means "from the earth" or "low" or "lowly." It is derived from *humus*, meaning "earth" or "ground" or "soil." We could say that the humble are "down to earth."

We commonly think of people who carry themselves with a certain modesty, unpretentiousness, and courtesy as being humble—as opposed to being arrogant or pretentious or rude. Sometimes people from poor or working-class backgrounds are also described as being from humble origins—as opposed to wealth or privilege. And so humility has associations not only with a certain interior attitude or disposition of the heart, but also with lower economic or social status in the order of things. In the Beatitudes there is mention of both the poor and the poor in spirit. The poor are clearly those who suffer material poverty, but poor in spirit is more broadly suggestive of an inner sense of spiritual humility, regardless of economic or social position. According to the Gospels, both were considered blessed by Jesus.

This chapter explores a number of ways to understand what it means to walk humbly. Humility is a virtue to be cultivated in our thoughts, words, and actions through spiritual practice. We can also learn humility through personal suffering. For privileged people, another essential way to learn humility is through regular personal contact and solidarity with people who are poor.

HUMILITY AND AUTHENTICITY

True humility is related to authenticity. It is grounded in the truth of who we are. It does not exaggerate our importance or abilities, but neither does it diminish our goodness or gifts. "Pride makes us artificial," writes Thomas Merton, "and humility makes us real."[1]

The Merriam-Webster dictionary defines *humility* as "the quality or state of not thinking you are better than other people." In this sense the person with humility regards others as equals, while the person who lacks humility has a false sense of superiority. While it is certainly true that some people are more gifted or talented than others at certain things (for example, Albert Einstein at physics and Michael Jordan at basketball), it is simply not true that anyone is, in essence, superior to any other human being on the planet. This would be a lie. It was a lie if white slaveowners thought they were any better than the human beings they considered property, just as it is a lie for privileged persons

---

[1] Thomas Merton, *No Man Is an Island* (Boston: Shambhala Publications, 2005 <1955>), 119.

to think they are superior to individuals from the inner city, or for men to think they are superior to women. Albert Nolan writes about the relationship of humility and truth:

> Humility is a matter of truth, of recognizing the truth about yourself. To imagine that you are superior to other people when you are not, or inferior to others when you are not, would be to have a false image of yourself. Recognizing the truth about yourself entails recognizing the futility of all comparisons in terms of superior and inferior.[2]

Humility should not be confused with low self-esteem or neurotic feelings of inferiority, because these too are not based on an accurate appraisal of the truth of who we are. True humility is not based on disparaging or diminishing ourselves. It is grounded in a right love for ourselves as we actually are.

A good part of my work as a psychotherapist centers on helping people who suffer from feelings of shame and inferiority to develop a more compassionate attitude toward themselves. These issues can be particularly complex and challenging for those who are different in one way or another from whatever happens to be the prevailing idea of what is desirable or normal (body image, sexual orientation, skin color, and so forth). For example, in my work with gay men, sometimes the crucial healing task in their process of "coming out" has been simply to acknowledge and accept the God-given fact of who they are. This is easier said than done, and it is even harder to do when prevailing prejudices in church and society create doubts about whether one is worthy of unconditional acceptance and respect.

Disrespect and discrimination in any context can make people vulnerable to toxic feelings of shame and doubt about their

---

[2] Albert Nolan, *Jesus Today: A Spirituality of Radical Freedom* (Maryknoll, NY: Orbis Books, 2006), 120.

fundamental worth and goodness. At its deepest level, this is a spiritual wound. "One of the most blasphemous consequences of injustice and prejudice," writes Desmond Tutu, "is that it can make a child of God doubt that he or she is a child of God."[3]

It is also important to distinguish true humility from the pretense of humility. If we are actually gifted or talented in a certain way, it does no one any good to pretend that we are not. At best, such lack of authenticity is annoying. At worst, when false humility inhibits or prevents a person from developing his or her potential or fully using his or her talents or gifts, the world is a poorer place because it has been deprived of the unique contribution that person could have made.

People who are openly arrogant or narcissistic are transparent in their lack of humility, but others may try to conceal their egocentrism behind a mask or persona of false humility. Egocentrism can be seen as a kind of psychological equivalent or parallel to the spiritual concept of sin. On a psychological level the sin of pride or *hubris* refers to the arrogance of setting up our own ego in the place of God.[4] In this sense egocentrism is analogous to idolatry.

We can and should try to cultivate the virtue of humility through spiritual practice, but there are limits to what can be accomplished through our own efforts. Nolan offers a realistic perspective:

You cannot become humble by merely deciding to do so. No amount of determination and will power will make you humble. The harder you try, the less you are likely to

---

[3] Desmond Tutu, *God Has a Dream* (New York: Doubleday, 2004), 40.

[4] For some helpful perspective on the psychology and spirituality of egocentrism and sin, see John Sanford, *Healing Body and Soul: The Meaning of Illness in the New Testament and in Psychotherapy* (Louisville, KY: Westminster/John Knox, 1992).

succeed, because this kind of effort will be the work of your ego.

What you can do is become more aware of your pride or lack of humility—of your ego.[5]

True humility, it seems, does not result from the strivings of our own egos. Ultimately, it is the fruit of self-knowledge. On a psychological level it flows from a humbling awareness of the damaging effects of our own egocentrism and lack of authenticity and from a perceived need to get back into right relationship with ourselves and others. On a spiritual level it flows from a humbling acknowledgment of our own sinfulness and a felt need to get right with God.

WHERE THE LADDERS START

Spatial metaphors for humility point *downward*. The haughty look *down* on those who they feel are beneath them; the humble walk with their feet on the ground, aware that they are human like everybody else. The wealthy and powerful move in well-connected circles at the top of the social hierarchy; the lowly and downtrodden do the best they can at the bottom of the social ladder. We can be humbled or brought low by all kinds of inner pain or outer trouble.

There is a beautiful poem titled "The Circus Animals' Desertion" by the great Irish poet William Butler Yeats. He apparently wrote the poem after a period of great discouragement during which he could find no inspiration or compelling image with which to craft a poem. "I sought a theme and sought for it in vain," Yeats writes in frustration, "I sought it daily for six weeks or so." He tried to climb out of his uninspired rut through his own cleverness and verbal adeptness, which are represented by

---

[5] Nolan, *Jesus Today*, 120.

the "circus animals," but his efforts were to no avail; the circus
animals had deserted him. Finally, feeling defeated, he surren-
dered. He stopped trying so hard and simply allowed himself to
sink into his own desolation and dejection. "Maybe at last," he
writes, "being but a broken man, I must be satisfied with my
heart." His "ladder" was gone:

> Now that my ladder's gone,
> I must lie down where all the ladders start
> In the foul rag and bone shop of the heart.[6]

The "foul rag and bone shop of the heart" is a striking image
of the dark, messy world of our own inner experience, particularly as we encounter it during periods of personal anguish
or emotional pain. At such times we are reminded of our own
weakness, vulnerability, and lack of control over emotional states
or life problems that cannot easily be overcome by the power of
our own will. Even Yeats could not *make* himself be inspired to
write a poem. People who are suffering from anxiety or depression are not always able simply to snap out of it—or *climb* out of
it—through their own efforts. Similarly, those who suffer from
alcoholism sometimes reach a point when they can no longer
deny having a problem. Try as they might, they realize that they
are simply unable to stop drinking on their own. They have "hit
bottom."

Hitting bottom, sinking into the place "where all the ladders
start," can feel like giving up on ourselves. We fight the inclination to surrender because it represents a defeat for our ego. But
sometimes there is nothing we *can* do; outer events or inner pain
bring us to our knees. It feels like the beginning of the end. We
may enter a hellish place of personal despair, over which hangs

---

[6] W. B. Yeats, "The Circus Animals' Desertion," in *The Collected Poems of
W. B. Yeats,* ed. Richard J. Finneran (New York: Scribner, 1996), 346–47.

the sign from Dante's *Inferno*: "Abandon all hope, ye who enter here." There is not always a redemptive outcome, and so we must be careful not to romanticize or spiritualize the suffering of the soul. The pain may be too much to bear. In one way or another, many give up.

For some, though, what looks like defeat can become an occasion for spiritual awakening and a new beginning. Yeats found rich images and inspiration for new poetry in the dreaded rag and bone shop of his own heart. In Alice Walker's book *The Color Purple*, a soulful blues singer named Shug speaks eloquently of the spiritual potential of sorrow and trouble:

> Here's the thing. . . . The thing I believe. God is inside you and inside everybody else. You come into the world with God. But only them that search inside for it find it. And sometimes it just manifest itself even if you not looking, or don't know what you looking for. Trouble do it for most folks, I think. Sorrow, Lord. Feeling like shit.[7]

Sorrow and trouble serve as a humbling reality check for our own ego. They remind us that we are not God, and they put us in touch with our need for someone or something other than ourselves to save and heal us from whatever is ailing us. In psychotherapy the process of honestly acknowledging and grappling with our emotional pain in the context of a therapeutic relationship can lead to a breakthrough of healing and liberating insight. Where before we saw only darkness and chaos, now it becomes possible to see patterns and themes; we begin to discern the "myth in the mess" of our own life. In Twelve Step programs, after people take the humbling first step of recognizing their alcoholism, they then must acknowledge their need for the help of

---

[7] Alice Walker, *The Color Purple* (New York: Washington Square Press, 1982), 177.

a power greater than themselves to restore them to sanity, which becomes crucial in their ongoing process of recovery.

Moral anguish is another form of pain that humbles us. We experience it through what is traditionally called the sting of conscience. Pangs of guilt or regret or shame cause us to wince inwardly over real or imagined sins, things we have done or things we think we could or should have done. In my psychotherapeutic work I spend considerable time helping people to examine such feelings. It is always crucial to differentiate between *neurotic guilt* (needless anxious preoccupation with imagined sins) and *real guilt* (over harm that has actually been done) for which we really need forgiveness. This includes what is known as existential guilt, which arises from our own lack of authenticity and evasion of responsibility in matters of calling and conscience. It takes real courage to take an honest look at such feelings, which are often embarrassing to acknowledge to ourselves and others. Such self-knowledge helps us to be humble, and it also helps us to be less judgmental of others.

Paradoxically, by drawing us downward and inward into ourselves, our pain can soften and deepen us, making us more compassionate and sensitive to the pain of others. Along these lines there is a beautiful passage from Chaim Potok's novel *The Chosen*. One of the characters, an Orthodox rabbi named Reb Saunders, is recalling some important life lessons he learned from his father:

> One learns of the pain of others by suffering one's own pain, he would say, by turning inside oneself, by finding one's own soul. And it is important to know of pain, he said. It destroys our self-pride, our arrogance, our indifference toward others. It makes us aware of how frail and tiny we are and of how much we must depend on the Master of the Universe.[8]

---

[8] Chaim Potok, *The Chosen* (New York: Fawcett Crest, 1967), 265.

Pride is characterized by a false sense of superiority that is based on a denial of "how frail and tiny we are" in the scheme of things. It is also based on a kind of pseudo-independence based on a denial of our *need* for others—including God. If we set up our own ego in the place of God, we live under the illusion that we do not have to depend upon anyone but ourselves. This way of being and thinking may work to some degree when things are going our way. But it is inevitably put to the test by sorrow and trouble, which push us to recognize our need for help from someone or something beyond ourselves. This could be a friend, a family member, a professional, a community, or even the "Master of the Universe."

Ultimately, humility comes from feeling and knowing our personal need for God. We are not called to walk alone; Micah says we are called to walk humbly *with our God* (Mi 6:8).

THE POOR AND THE POOR IN SPIRIT

There are two versions of what have come to be known as the Beatitudes, one in the Gospel of Matthew (5:1–12) and the other in the Gospel of Luke (6:20–26). There are clear similarities and parallels between the two texts but also some notable differences.

Both Gospels contain a series of statements about those whom Jesus considered "blessed." Luke's list is shorter: the poor; the hungry; those who weep; and those who are hated, excluded, reviled, and defamed. Matthew's list is a little longer and more inclusive: the poor in spirit, those who mourn, the meek, those who hunger and thirst for righteousness, the merciful, the pure in heart, the peacemakers, and those who are reviled and persecuted for righteousness's sake. In Luke the Beatitudes are actually called the Blessings and Woes because, for every blessing, there is a complementary woe or warning. For example, "Blessed are you who are poor" is paired with "But *woe* to you who are rich."

Luke's descriptions of the blessed are more concrete. They are simply the "poor" or those "who are hungry now," whereas Matthew describes them more figuratively as the "poor in spirit" or "those who hunger and thirst for righteousness":

Blessed are you who are poor, for yours is the kingdom of God.	Blessed are the poor in spirit, for theirs is the kingdom of heaven.
Blessed are you who are hungry now, for you will be filled.	Blessed are those who hunger and thirst for righteousness, for they will be filled.
(Lk 6:20–21)	(Mt 5:3, 6)

In the effort to understand what it means to be humble, the distinct but overlapping meanings of "poor" and "poor in spirit" are worth exploring. In Luke, it seems clear that "you who are poor" refers to people who are suffering in actual material poverty. The poor are humble because they have little or nothing in the way of money or security or status. Similarly, "Blessed are you who are hungry now" leaves no doubt that Jesus was talking about people who literally do not get enough to eat. The Greek word for "poor" used in both Luke and Matthew, *ptochoi*, is suggestive of extreme neediness. Specifically, it refers to the undignified manner of destitute persons who "stoop" or "cower" as they beg for food.

Jesus seemed to have a special fondness for needy people, those who were regarded as unimportant and unworthy of respect in his culture. He referred to them as the "least" and the "last." Eduardo Galeano calls them the "nobodies":

The nobodies: nobody's children, owners of nothing. The nobodies: the no ones, the nobodied, running like rabbits, dying through life, screwed every which way.[9]

---

[9] Eduardo Galeano, "The Nobodies," in *The Book of Embraces* (New York: W. W. Norton, 1989), 73.

The poor tend to be seen as inferior or cursed because they are in an inferior social position. They are not actually inferior, of course, which is one reason Jesus sticks up for them and calls them blessed. The nobodies, who count for nothing in the eyes of the world, are somebodies in the eyes of God. "So the last will be first, and the first will be last" (Mt 20:16). Jesus grew up in the prophetic tradition that emphasized justice and compassion for the poor, but he went even further by adding "that God is *in* the poor, that we directly encounter God in the poor, and that how we treat the poor is how we treat him."[10]

Matthew's use of "poor in spirit" in place of Luke's "poor" is controversial. The concern, at least among some interpreters, is that Matthew may have spiritualized or softened the original saying of Jesus, thereby shifting the focus from the objective pain and need of those who suffer in unjust poverty to a subjective, interior quality of spiritual humility. Others disagree with this interpretation of Matthew, including none other than Gustavo Gutiérrez, the father of liberation theology.[11] After all, it is Matthew who includes the story of the Last Judgment in his Gospel, in which Jesus states quite plainly that we will all ultimately be held accountable for how we have treated the *least* of our brothers and sisters during our lifetime in this world (Mt 25:31–46).

Gutiérrez believes that "poor in spirit" is actually suggestive of a radical kind of discipleship and solidarity with the poor. In the context of the other beatitudes in Matthew, those who are poor in spirit are also presumed to be hungering and thirsting for righteousness, performing the works of mercy, making peace,

---

[10] Ronald Rolheiser, *Sacred Fire: A Vision for a Deeper Human and Christian Maturity* (New York: Image Books, 2014).

[11] See Gustavo Gutiérrez, "Option for the Poor," in *Systematic Theology: Perspectives from Liberation Theology,* ed. Jon Sobrino and Ignacio Ellacuría, 22–37 (Maryknoll, NY: Orbis Books, 1993). See also Gustavo Gutiérrez, "The Church of the Beatitudes," in *Gustavo Gutiérrez: Essential Writings,* ed. James B. Nickoloff, 162–65 (Maryknoll, NY: Orbis Books, 1996).

and perhaps even taking risks on behalf of the poor that could result in being persecuted or getting into serious trouble for righteousness's sake. In many places around the world, identifying with the cause of the poor can be a life-and-death matter.

To speak of spirits, or of being "in" a certain spirit, is an ancient way of referring to inner dynamics or inclinations operating within the human person. This is not necessarily suggestive of a belief in invisible spirits that have the power to possess or take control of a person. Such beliefs were common in the ancient world at the time of Jesus, as evidenced by a number of gospel stories about demonic possession and exorcism. Some modern people also use the language of good and evil spirits to describe their day-to-day process of discernment and making choices. Over five hundred years ago Saint Ignatius Loyola developed a psychologically sophisticated model for the discernment of spirits that is still found very useful in many circles today.

Spirits are also seen in the Bible as reflecting fundamental dispositions of the human heart. People can be "in" one kind of spirit or another. For example, in Proverbs a distinction is drawn between the "haughty spirit" of the proud and the "lowly spirit" of the poor:

> Pride goes before destruction,
>> and a haughty spirit before a fall.
> It is better to be of a lowly spirit among the
>> poor
>> than to divide the spoil with the proud. (Prv
>> 16:18–19)

Here, the "haughty spirit" represents a disposition to arrogance and selfishness and greed ("dividing the spoil with the proud"), which is a set up for inevitable defeat and downfall.

The "lowly spirit" is preferable. Such a spirit is clearly suggestive of something more fundamental than a mood or feeling; to be of a lowly spirit is not the same as feeling low or depressed, or in poor spirits, or feeling poorly about oneself. The lowly spirit is associated with the poor. Persons characterized by such a spirit are not ashamed to be poor and humble, or to be associated with the poor and humble. This is likely much closer to what it means to be "poor in spirit."

In a similar spirit, but from a different tradition, there is a lovely poem by Han-shan, a ninth-century Zen Buddhist poet. He lived a reclusive, austere life in a mountainous area of China known as Cold Mountain. Han-shan apparently wrote the poem after being mocked by someone about his poetry and the simplicity of his lifestyle:

> Someone criticized the Master of Cold Moun-
> tain:
> "Your poems make no sense at all."
> "But from what I have read of the ancients,"
> I said,
> "They weren't ashamed to be poor and hum-
> ble."
> He laughed at my words and answered,
> "How can you talk such foolishness?"
> Then go on, my friend, as you are today.
> Let money be your whole life for you![12]

Conventional cultural expectations measure success by the yardstick of upward mobility, the idea that we should always be climbing up the social ladder toward greater achievement, status, privilege, honor, and financial security. For the privileged the obsessive pursuit of "more" can become a distraction not only from the uncomfortable reality of social suffering all around us,

---

[12] See *Cold Mountain: 100 Poems by the T'ang Poet Han-shan*, trans. Burton Watson (New York: Columbia University Press, 1970), 73.

but from our own spiritual emptiness and existential need. It seems only right that the poor should be able to escape from unjust poverty to a more decent standard of living. For the privileged, however, upward mobility can represent, in some cases, an anxious escape or flight *from* the poor—and from ourselves. Instead of becoming genuinely humble or poor in spirit, we are spiritually impoverished. The only cure for this is regular time away from the rat race of upward mobility, and regular personal contact with people who are poor and humble.

Personal encounters with people in situations of poverty and oppression can awaken our social conscience and clarify our priorities about what is truly important. The poor move from being a vague abstraction and become particular persons and communities that are hurting in particular ways. Callings to compassionate service and lasting commitments to social justice can only grow out of such personal contact with real persons and the distressing social realities in which they live. Referring to our passage from Micah, Jon Sobrino writes of the deep and potentially transformative spiritual potential of such encounters:

> The encounter with the poor is a spiritual experience, an experience of God. In these terms the proclamation of Micah acquires its historical logic. As we stand before the poor, as we stand before the crucified peoples, the demand becomes utterly clear, to practice justice and to love with tenderness. In this fashion one walks with God in history, humbly.[13]

Jesus seemed particularly drawn toward humble people at the bottom of the social ladder. Contrary to the expected upward trajectory, there was a markedly countercultural trend in his

---

[13] Jon Sobrino, "Spirituality and the Following of Jesus," in Sobrino and Ellacuría, *Systematic Theology*, 256.

life toward *downward mobility*. His heart inclined him to move toward—rather than away from—the despised and rejected. He loved them and was not ashamed to be associated with them. Jesus seemed to identify with people in his society who lacked dignity. This is perhaps most poignantly exemplified in the undignified manner of his own death, by which he personally experienced—like countless other "nobodies" in his society—what it was like to be persecuted, reviled, and tortured. "The divine way," writes Henri Nouwen, "is indeed the downward way."[14]

Ignatius Loyola saw Jesus as the perfect embodiment of what he called loving humility (in Spanish, *humildad amorosa*), which he saw as the ultimate climax or fulfillment of the spiritual journey for followers of Jesus.[15]

In order to imitate Christ our Lord better and to be more like him here and now, I desire and choose poverty with Christ poor rather than wealth; contempt with Christ laden with it rather than honors. Even further, I desire to be regarded as a useless fool for Christ, who before me was regarded as such, rather than as a wise or prudent person in this world.[16]

It is evident that such profound humility requires tremendous courage, even heroism. To be sure, not everyone is called to such heroism. But *some* are, and the rest of us must look to them for inspiration. All of us, though, are called to become ever more humble, decent, and loving persons while we have the chance.

---

[14] Henri Nouwen, *The Selfless Way of Christ: Downward Mobility and the Spiritual Life* (Maryknoll, NY: Orbis Books, 2007), 23.

[15] See George Ganss, SJ, commentary on "Three Ways of Being Humble," in *The Spiritual Exercises of Saint Ignatius: A Translation and Commentary* (St. Louis: Institute of Jesuit Sources, 1992), 173–76.

[16] *The Spiritual Exercises of Saint Ignatius,* 73.

LEARNING TO KNEEL

We can be brought to our knees by all kinds of inner pain and outer trouble. Suffering can humiliate us, break us down, make us numb and self-centered. But it can also evoke the deepest and best in us and teach us humility by helping us to recognize our need for God. It all depends on our attitude. Life can certainly force us to our knees in humiliation and defeat, but it is also possible to make a conscious choice to kneel in prayer and surrender. The most beautiful example I can think of is the story of Etty Hillesum.

Esther Hillesum (1914–43) was a young Jewish woman from the Netherlands who died at Auschwitz in November 1943. Her diaries and letters offer a remarkable account of her inner experiences during the German occupation of her homeland. Covering the period from March 1941 to September 1943, they give evidence of her keen capacity to observe the inner movements of her own soul, her deep and unconventional spirituality, and her courageous and compassionate witness to the social catastrophe of the Holocaust.[17] Over a period of just two and one-half years, Etty experienced a profound spiritual transformation marked by an ever-deepening sense of prayerful connection and humble surrender to God.[18] In her own way Etty embodied a deep sense of loving humility during her short, interrupted life.

Etty was an insecure and troubled soul with a mystical bent. She came from a highly educated but unhappy family; she referred to her home as "the madhouse." Her family was culturally

---

[17] See Etty Hillesum, *Etty: The Letters and Diaries of Etty Hillesum 1941–1943* (Grand Rapids, MI: Eerdmans, 2002). For an excellent short biography of Etty Hillesum (and an edited sampling of her writings) see Annemarie S. Kidder, "Introduction," *Etty Hillesum: Essential Writings*, ed. Annemarie S. Kidder, 1–24 (Maryknoll, NY: Orbis Books, 2009). See also Etty Hillesum, *An Interrupted Life* and *Letters from Westerbork* (New York: Henry Holt, 1996).

[18] See Patrick Woodhouse, *Etty Hillesum: A Life Transformed* (London: Bloomsbury Academic, 2009).

Jewish, but it seems she received little in the way of religious formation in Judaism as a child. Her physical and emotional health were fragile, and she was vulnerable to bouts of fatigue and dark depression. In her early twenties she tended to move in heady intellectual and left-wing circles. She was romantic and prone to emotionally intense, turbulent relationships with men; in her diaries she acknowledges having had sexual relationships with a number of lovers. Etty's candor about her love life along with her unconventional spirituality may be reasons her writings have received less attention than other modern autobiographies and Holocaust literature (for example, Anne Frank, also from Amsterdam, is the author of the most famous diary of all time).

In March 1941, at a time she described herself as "nothing more or less than a miserable, frightened creature," Etty sought professional help for her emotional and relational problems from Julius Spier, a psycho-chirologist (an unusual blend of psycho-analysis and palm reading) who had received personal training from C. G. Jung. Some of Spier's unorthodox therapeutic methods seem odd, and the confusion of personal and professional boundaries in his relationship with Etty would be unacceptable today. Nonetheless, it is clear that her therapeutic work with him had a profoundly stabilizing, formative, and healing impact on her life. It was Spier who encouraged Etty to develop her practice of contemplative inward listening and prayer. He was also responsible for suggesting that she begin to keep a journal or "exercise book" about her inner life, a practice she took up quite religiously after their first meeting. Ten of these books survive; an unfinished journal that Etty took with her on the train to Auschwitz has been lost.

"What a strange story it really is," Etty wrote in one exercise book, "my story: the girl who could not kneel. Or its variation: the girl who learned to pray."[19] She made many entries about her

---

[19] *Etty: The Letters and Diaries of Etty Hillesum 1941–1943,* 547.

personal struggles with prayer, a humbling process she likened
to "learning to kneel." Kneeling became the central metaphor
for her spiritual life. At one point she thought of writing a story
about "the girl who could not kneel" or "the girl who gradu-
ally learned to kneel."[20] Etty identified a number of reasons that
kneeling was challenging and even embarrassing for her:

> Kneeling doesn't really come easily to me. I feel a sort of
> embarrassment. Why? Probably because of the critical, ra-
> tional, atheistic bit that is part of me as well. And yet every
> so often I have a great urge to kneel down with my face in
> my hands and in this way to find some peace and to listen
> to that hidden source within me.[21]

Even more powerful than her intellectual resistance to prayer
was the sense of personal vulnerability Etty felt in her relationship with God, whom she sometimes experienced as an invisible
lover who could be unsettlingly intimate and close. "That [kneel-
ing] is my most intimate gesture," she writes, "more intimate
even than being with a man."[22]

> Last night, shortly before going to bed, I suddenly went
> down on my knees in the middle of this large room, be-
> tween the steel chairs and the matting. Almost automatical-
> ly. Forced to the ground by something stronger than myself.
> Some time ago I told myself "I am a kneeler in training."
> I was still embarrassed by this act, as intimate as gestures
> of love that cannot be put into words, except by a poet.[23]

---

[20] Ibid., 148.
[21] Ibid., 103.
[22] Ibid., 547.
[23] Ibid., 181.

Though Etty was not a traditionally religious person in any way, God became profoundly real to her over the last two years or so of her short life. Being who she was, she also consistently maintained a certain skepticism about her mystical connection with God, whom she once described as "the deepest and best within me."[24] Her view of God resembled that of Jung, who saw the deep inner self as something like the psychological equivalent of God.

> When I pray, . . . I hold a silly, naive, or deadly serious dialogue with what is deepest inside me, which for the sake of convenience I call God.[25]

The inner dialogue became deadly serious as extreme anti-Jewish measures taken by the Nazis intensified (wearing identifying yellow stars, restrictions on movement and housing, violent abuse, arbitrary arrests, and so forth). As time went on the focus of Etty's reflections began to shift from her love life and private inner experiences of prayer to the terrifying social reality of occupation and persecution.

> More arrests, more terror, concentration camps, the arbitrary dragging off of fathers, sisters, brothers. . . . Everything seems so menacing and ominous, and always that feeling of total impotence.[26]

For Etty, prayer became a necessity—both to hold herself together and to protect her inner being from the toxic effects of mounting evil:

----

[24] Ibid., 83.
[25] Ibid., 494.
[26] Ibid., 62.

The threat grows ever greater, and terror increases from day to day. I draw prayer round me like a dark protective wall, withdraw inside it as one might into a convent cell and then step outside again, calmer and stronger and more collected again. . . . I can imagine times to come when I shall stay on my knees for days on end waiting until the protective walls are strong enough to prevent my going to pieces all together, my being lost and utterly devastated.[27]

In July 1942, the systematic removal of Jews from Amsterdam began. After being rounded up, they were sent to the Westerbork "transit" camp north of Amsterdam. Over 100,000 Jewish men, women, and children (including Anne Frank and Edith Stein) were temporarily detained in hellish conditions at Westerbork prior to being deported to concentration camps in Poland. Etty realized that it was only a matter of time before she would be called upon to share the "common destiny" of her people.

For a time Etty was spared having to go to Westerbork. She was appointed to a job with the Jewish Council, a group that worked in collaboration with the Nazis to assist with the administrative task of organizing the removal of Jews. She took the job with deep misgivings: "Nothing can ever atone," she writes with shame and regret, "for the fact that one section of the Jewish population is helping to transport the majority out of the country."[28] She quickly requested a transfer to the Social Welfare for People in Transit department at Westerbork, which would at least allow her to minister directly to the needs of fellow Jews in this impossible situation. For the first year or so Etty's presence at the camp was voluntary, and she was occasionally allowed to go back and forth to Amsterdam. But she would eventually lose

---

[27] Ibid., 364.
[28] Ibid., 511.

this privilege and become a detained "person in transit" herself. Friends offered to use their connections to find a hiding place for her, but she declined.

The situation at Westerbork became increasingly overcrowded and desperate. "What we have now," Etty writes in a letter to a friend, "is a complete catastrophe." The camp had been "engulfed by successive tidal waves of Jews."[29] The barracks became

> a jam-packed human warehouse: people sleeping three to a bed in narrow iron bunks, no mattresses for the men, nowhere at all to store anything, children terrified and screaming, the greatest possible wretchedness.[30]

People waited in unbearable suspense for word about when they would be loaded on trains bound for ominous destinations "in the East." She describes helping people prepare for the dreaded train:

> Tonight I shall be helping to dress babies and to calm mothers—and that is all I can hope to do. I could almost curse myself for that. For all we know we are yielding up our sick and defenseless brothers and sisters to hunger, heat, cold, exposure, and destruction, and yet we dress and escort them to the bare cattle cars—and if they can't walk we carry them on stretchers. What is going on, what mysteries are these, in what sort of fatal mechanism have we become enmeshed?[31]

In June 1943, Etty witnessed the arrival of her parents and her brother Mischa at Westerbork:

---

[29] Ibid., 604.
[30] Ibid.
[31] Ibid., 645.

The jam-packed freight train drew into the camp this morning. I stood beside it in the rain. The cars were shut tight, but there were a few small openings here and there high up, where the planks had been broken. Through one of these I suddenly saw Mother's hat and Father's glasses and Mischa's peaky face. I started to shout and they saw me. Now I shall have to share the same torture with them. . . . Suddenly it's all coming to an end.[32]

Old emotional strains and hurts and resentments in her relationships with her parents seemed to soften and melt away in the final months that Etty spent with them at Westerbork. She became preoccupied with finding ways to show kindness by making them more comfortable in a terrible situation. "Thanks to the many friends I have here, it'll be possible to make life easier for them in all sorts of small ways."[33]

In the extremity of Westerbork, Etty's sense of vocation, which she called her "destiny," seemed to deepen and clarify in important ways. "Instead of living an accidental life," she writes, "you feel deep down that you have grown mature enough to accept your 'destiny.'"[34]

First, in such a loveless place, it is clear that she experienced a calling to be a loving, merciful, compassionate presence to others. "They are merciless, totally without pity," she writes of the heartless Nazi bureaucrats and jeering guards. "And we must be all the more merciful ourselves."[35] A deep, aching, spiritual tenderness was evoked in Etty by the suffering at Westerbork: "I love people so terribly," she writes, addressing God, "because in every human being I love something of You."[36]

---

[32] Ibid., 604.
[33] Ibid.
[34] Ibid., 359.
[35] Ibid., 497.
[36] Ibid., 514.

The natural self-protective inclination to preserve one's sanity in such a situation is to become emotionally and spiritually numb. Etty resisted this and tried instead to remain a conscious, thoughtful, feeling witness:

> What I fear most is numbness, and all those people with whom I shall be herded together. And yet there must be someone to live through it all and bear witness to the fact that God lived, even in these times. And why should I not be that witness?[37]

She prayed that she could become what she calls "the thinking heart of the barracks":

> At night, as I lay in the camp on my plank bed, surrounded by women and girls snoring, dreaming aloud, quietly sobbing and tossing and turning, women and girls who often told me during the day, "We don't want to think, we don't want to feel, otherwise we are sure to go out of our minds," I was sometimes filled with an infinite tenderness, and lay awake for hours letting all the many, too many impressions of a much-too-long day wash over me, and I prayed, "Let me be the thinking heart of these barracks."[38]

Etty knew the best way she could personally serve as a witness was to use her talent with words; she could document all that she was seeing and feeling and experiencing.

> If I have one real duty in life, in these times, at this stage of my life, then it is to write, to record, to retain.[39]

---

[37] Ibid., 506.
[38] Ibid., 542–43.
[39] Ibid., 537.

And I shall wield this slender fountain pen as if it were a
hammer, and my words will have to be so many hammer
strokes with which to beat out the story of our fate and of
a piece of history as it is and never was before.[40]

Etty's many exquisitely written letters are not only indica-
tive of faithfulness to relationships with friends and loved ones,
but they also are evidence of faithfulness to her calling. And by
making sure to preserve her diaries (she gave them to a friend
with the request that they might one day be published), she
was preserving not only her personal memories, but she was
bearing witness to the historical memory of her people and to
"the fact that God lived, even in these times." Etty's last bit of
writing was on a postcard to her friend Christine van Nooten.
Dated September 7, 1943, she threw it from a train bound for
Auschwitz, where she died less than three months later at the age
of twenty-nine. The card was found by farmers near the tracks:

Christine,
    Opening the Bible at random I find this: "The Lord is
my high tower." I am sitting on a rucksack in the middle
of a full freight car. Father, Mother, and Mischa are a few
cars away. In the end, the departure came without warning. On special orders from the Hague. We left the camp
singing, Father and Mother firmly and calmly, Mischa too.
. . . Goodbye for now from the four of us.
    Etty[41]

We left the camp singing. Where does such bravery and dignity come from? I suspect that Etty would say it was the fruit
of prayer, that it came from learning to pray or, in her words,

---

[40] Ibid., 484.
[41] Ibid., 658–59.

learning to kneel. "I have had to learn it the hard way," she once said—before she really knew how terribly hard things were going to get.

> I think that I can bear everything life and these times have in store for me. And when the turmoil becomes too great and I am completely at my wits' end, then I still have my folded hands and bended knee.[42]

Etty was reminding herself that she could always turn to prayer, no matter what. Prayer had become an invisible lifeline to the deepest and best within her: God. When the time came for the ultimate test, she hoped she could hang on. She did. And God lived, even then.

---

[42] Ibid., 547.

EPILOGUE

All the great experiences of life—freedom, encounter, love,
death—are worked out in the silent turbulence of an impov-
erished spirit. A gentleness comes over us when we confront
such decisive moments. We are quietly but deeply moved by
a mature encounter; we become suddenly humble when we
are overtaken by love. . . .

The reason is that in such experiences the moment of
truth arrives; our life and our being are revealed to us. . . .
We dimly begin to realize that we are poor, that our power
and strength are derived from the wellsprings of invisible
mystery.

—Johannes Baptist Metz,
Poverty of Spirit

OVER THE YEARS I have often sought the advice and perspective of my older brother, Jim Neafsey, especially on important
matters of conscience and calling. He embodies for me the kind
of person who was known in early Irish monasticism as an *anam*
cara or "soul friend."[1] A year or so ago, when I told Jim about my
idea of writing a book about Micah and vocation, he suggested

---

[1] John O'Donohue, *Anam Cara: A Book of Celtic Wisdom* (New York: Harper
Perennial, 1998).

that I consider justice, love, and humility as interrelated and
integral dimensions of one essential human calling—"like three
facets of one unnameable Mystery of life" was the way he put
it. In his own lyrical, mystical way, Jim wrote:

> Walking humbly with God is, I think, ultimately identical
> with acting justly and loving tenderly. Walking humbly
> with God is the result of having one's mind blown by the
> Mystery and having one's heart broken and broken open by
> life in its beautiful and terrifying reality. You are no longer
> striving to be humble. You have been radically humbled by
> life and by the Mystery.[2]

Etty Hillesum's heart was certainly broken by the cruel circumstances of her life, but it was also *broken open* to reveal the
profound depths of loving humility and compassion in her complex, beautiful soul. Like it or not, and sooner or later, all of us
are inevitably brought to our knees by one form of heartbreak
or another. Whether or not we learn to kneel is another story.
Sorrow and trouble can break us down, but they can also create
the conditions for spiritual breakthrough. It all depends on our
attitude.

Experiences of personal suffering, or close encounters with
the pain of others, have the potential to put us in touch with
the sacred dimension of experience from which callings emerge.
After six Jesuits from the University of Central America were
murdered by the Salvadoran army in 1989, an American Jesuit
named Dean Brackley (1946–2011) felt moved to volunteer to
go to El Salvador to try to fill the vacuum of Jesuit leadership in
that place so stricken by injustice and violence. For many years

---

[2] James M. Neafsey, personal communication, April 21, 2015. Jim and his
wife, Carmen, have served as spiritual directors in Berkeley, California, for many
years.

Brackley hosted delegations of American visitors to El Salvador, making sure the visitors had many opportunities to hear humble Salvadoran people share their personal stories of hardship and resilience. Brackley came to believe that the most important and potentially life-changing thing that could happen on these trips was for the visitors' hearts to be broken. He wrote:

> As the humanity of the poor crashes through the visitors' defenses, they glimpse their reflection in the eyes of their hosts. ("These people are just like us!") They feel gently invited to lay down the burden of superiority of which they were scarcely aware. They are brushed with a light shame and confusion, and they feel they are losing their grip. Actually, it is the world that is losing its grip on them. I mean the world consisting of important people like them-selves and unimportant poor people. That world starts to unhinge. The experience threatens to sweep them out of control like a stream in spring. It is like the disorientation of falling in love. In fact, that is what is happening, a kind of falling in love.[3]

The stakes in these matters of the heart and soul seem to get higher as we grow older. My brother Jim adds: "It is, I think, one of the central calls of midlife and aging." Midlife is a rough marker for the beginning of what Jung referred to as "the second half of life," during which we tend to become increasingly conscious of our mortality and the question of what really matters during our short lives here on this earth. For Jung, the challenge of the second half of life is not only to make peace with our finitude, but also to find meaningful

---

[3] Dean Brackley, *The Call to Discernment in Troubled Times: New Perspectives on the Transformative Wisdom of Ignatius of Loyola* (New York: Crossroads, 2004), 35.

ways to connect to the infinite.[4] In the first half of life the task is getting established and finding a place in the world, but as life goes on it becomes more clear that we will ultimately have to let go of everything. The deeper needs and longings of the soul begin to call for attention.

The sense of mortality is sobering and humbling, but it can also be liberating and focusing. Instead of grief and regret over lost time and an unlived life, or resentment of our obligations, or despair over what we could do if only there were was enough time, it becomes possible to think about what *can* be done in the time we have left. The aim is to be useful, to give back, to do some good while we have the chance. The breakthrough of this kind of life-giving generativity has been referred to by Ronald Rolheiser as "mature discipleship," a way of living characterized by the inclination to give one's life away.[5]

So many inspiring examples come to mind. I think of one lovely immigrant family with a wheelchair-bound adult daughter who suffers from cerebral palsy. For years the father has chosen to work the night shift at a grocery store so that he can be available to care for his daughter while her mother goes off to work during the day. His body is often very tired, but his soul is at rest.

There is a cost to mature discipleship. Some are literally called upon to lay down their lives for the sake of love and justice. "There are some things so dear," said Martin Luther King, Jr., "some things so precious, some things so eternally true, that they are worth *dying* for."[6] Some battles are worth fighting whether

---

[4] See Carl Jung, "Psychotherapists of the Clergy," in C. G. Jung, *Modern Man in Search of a Soul* (New York: Harcourt Harvest, 1955). For a thoughtful book from a Jungian perspective, see James Hollis, *Finding Meaning in the Second Half of Life: How to Finally, Really Grow Up* (New York: Penguin, 2006).

[5] Ronald Rolheiser, *Sacred Fire: A Vision for a Deeper Human and Christian Maturity* (New York: Image Books, 2014).

[6] Rev. Dr. Martin Luther King, Jr., speech, Great March on Detroit, June 23, 1963.

we win or lose; some things are worth doing regardless of how they turn out. There is a beautiful example in the movie *Glory*, the story of the 54th Regiment of the Massachusetts Volunteer Infantry, the first all-black regiment in the Union Army during the Civil War. The night before the final battle at Fort Wagner, when it is certain that the unit will suffer devastating casualties because they will lead the charge, the African American soldiers gather around a fire to pray and sing and offer testimonies to encourage and catch courage from one another. One of them, Private Silas Trip, a runaway slave, knows full well what it is like to be treated as *less* than a man. He also knows full well that he will likely be killed in the morning. Haltingly, but with deep conviction, he says, "It ain't even matter much what happen tomorrow, 'cause we men, ain't we? We *men*."[7]

Most of us are not called upon to engage in prophetic public heroism or to endure the ultimate sacrifice of martyrdom for a just cause. But all of us are called to ordinary courage and personal generosity, which require the day-to-day inner sacrifice of egocentric concerns—a kind of daily *dying* to self in the interest of steadfast love for others over the long haul. According to Rabbi David Wolpe, Micah's "only this" may be the most understated "only" on record, simply because the ongoing call to justice, love, and humility is so immense and unrelenting. "Romantic single gestures grab attention and acquire the luster of heroism," says Wolpe, "but it is the daily, draining effort to be kind, to rise above pettiness, irritation, and limitation, that is truly arduous, and praiseworthy."[8]

---

[7] In the movie *Glory* (1989), the character of Private Silas Trip is played by actor Denzel Washington, who won an Academy Award for Best Supporting Actor for his performance.

[8] David J. Wolpe, *The Healer of Shattered Hearts: A Jewish View of God* (New York: Penguin, 1990), 114–15.

Our stubborn, fearful egos tend to throw up all kinds of obstacles to being just, loving, and humble. Nevertheless, God breaks through, sometimes in spite of us, and it is still possible to do some good. The paradox was poignantly expressed by Ignatius Loyola in a 1545 letter to Francis Borgia, one of his early Jesuit companions. "I see the whole of myself as an obstacle to God's work," writes Ignatius. "This consideration brings me the greatest and sweetest consolation, because I realize that God in his loveliness works so many good things through me."[9]

As long as we are honest with ourselves, humility tends to take care of itself. We can concentrate on being useful, on putting one foot in front of the other, and remember that God is walking with us every step of the way.

---

[9] Excerpted from Ignatius Loyola, Letter to Francis Borgia (1545). The quotation used here is from a paraphrase of that letter by Anthony DeMello, SJ, in *Seek God Everywhere: Reflections on the Spiritual Exercises of Saint Ignatius* (New York: Image/Doubleday, 2010), 108. A version of the entire letter can be found in *Letters of St. Ignatius of Loyola,* ed. William J. Young (Chicago: Loyola Press, 1959), 83–85.

SUGGESTED READING

THE PROPHETS AND JESUS

Daniel Berrigan, *Minor Prophets, Major Themes* **(Marion, SD: Fortkamp Publishing/Rose Hill Books, 1995).**
In this fascinating book Berrigan offers his unique, poetic, radical exegesis on the books of Micah and the other minor prophets.

Walter Brueggemann, *The Prophetic Imagination***, 2nd ed. (Minneapolis, MN: Fortress Press, 2001).**
This powerful book by the popular and prolific scripture scholar explores the unique capacities for prophetic criticism, imagination, compassion, and inspiration in the Hebrew prophets and Jesus of Nazareth.

Walter Brueggemann, Sharon Parks, and Thomas Groome, *To Act Justly, Love Tenderly, Walk Humbly: An Agenda for Ministers* **(New York: Paulist Press, 1986).**
In this short book three well-known scholars offer insightful reflections on Micah's triple summons to justice, love, and humility.

Abraham Joshua Heschel, *The Prophets* **(New York: Harper Perennial, 1962).**
Heschel's masterpiece is a moving exploration of the words of the prophets and the powerful inner experiences that gave rise to them.

Megan McKenna, *Prophets: Words of Fire* **(Maryknoll, NY: Orbis Books, 2010.**
A thoughtful, accessible introduction to the writings of the Hebrew prophets.

Albert Nolan, *Jesus before Christianity* **(Maryknoll, NY: Orbis Books, 1976/2001).**
A classic, beautiful book that explores what we know about the unique consciousness of Jesus in his own life and times prior to the development of the Christian movement.

VOCATION AND HUMAN DEVELOPMENT

Herbert Alphonso, SJ, *Discovering Your Personal Vocation: The Search for Meaning through the Spiritual Exercises* **(Mahwah, NJ: Paulist Press, 2001).**
An inspiring little book on discernment of personal vocation in the *Spiritual Exercises* of Saint Ignatius Loyola.

Dorothy C. Bass and Mark R. Schwehn, *Leading Lives That Matter: What We Should Do and Who We Should Be* **(Grand Rapids, MI: Eerdmanns, 2006).**
A rich, diverse collection of excerpts on vocation from texts drawn from fiction, autobiography, philosophy, and spirituality.

Kathleen A. Cahalan and Bonnie J. Miller-McLemore, eds., *Calling All Years Good: Vocation across the Lifespan* **(Grand Rapids, MI: Eerdmans, 2017).**
An edited volume of the writings of members of the *Seminar on Vocation across the Lifespan* at the Collegeville Institute for Ecumenical and Cultural Research, including chapters on vocation in childhood, adolescence, young and middle and later adulthood, and older adulthood.

Edward Hahnenberg, *Awakening Vocation: A Theology of Christian Call* **(Wilmington, DE: Michael Glazier, 2010).**
An excellent overview of the theology of vocation by a Catholic theologian.

James Hillman, *The Soul's Code: In Search of Character and Calling* **(New York: Random House, 1996).**
A rich, evocative exploration of calling from the perspective of depth psychology.

Gregg Levoy, *Callings: Finding and Following an Authentic Life* **(New York: Harmony Books, 1998).**
An accessible, imaginative book on vocational self-discovery that is particularly useful for nonreligious spiritual seekers.

John Neafsey, *A Sacred Voice Is Calling: Personal Vocation and Social Conscience* **(Maryknoll, NY: Orbis Books, 2006).**
An ecumenical, interfaith, interdisciplinary exploration of the link between vocation and social responsibility, integrating insights from spirituality, liberation theology, and contemporary psychology.

Parker Palmer, *Let Your Life Speak: Listening for the Voice of Vocation* **(San Francisco: Jossey-Bass, 1999).**
A beautifully written, soulful little book.

Sharon Daloz Parks, *Big Questions, Worthy Dreams: Mentoring Emerging Adults in Their Search for Meaning, Purpose, and Faith* **(San Francisco: Jossey-Bass, 2011).**
An excellent, interdisciplinary book on vocational discernment and self-discovery in the lives of emerging adults, integrating insights from developmental psychology and faith development.

Ronald Rolheiser, *Sacred Fire: A Vision for a Deeper Human and Christian Maturity* **(New York: Image Books, 2014).**
A wise, compassionate book on the path of mature discipleship over the course of a lifetime.

SPIRITUALITY
AND SOCIAL CONCERN

Gregory Boyle, *Tattoos on the Heart: The Power of Boundless Compassion* **(New York: Free Press, 2010).**
A lovely, inspiring memoir by a priest who has devoted his life to redemptive work with young people caught up in the violent world of urban gangs.

Dean Brackley, *The Call to Discernment in Troubled Times: New Perspectives on the Transformative Wisdom of Ignatius of Loyola* **(New York: Crossroads, 2004).**
A moving, contemporary interpretation of Ignatian spirituality in the context of global inequity and injustice by an American Jesuit who volunteered to work in El Salvador after the murders of the Salvadoran Jesuits in 1989.

Gustavo Gutiérrez, *Gustavo Gutiérrez: Spiritual Writings,* **ed. Daniel G. Groody (Maryknoll, NY: Orbis Books, 2011).**
A great selection of the spiritual writings of the founder of liberation theology.

Elizabeth Johnson, *Quest for the Living God: Mapping Frontiers in the Theology of God* **(New York: Continuum, 2007).**
A scholarly, accessible, beautifully written book that masterfully reviews contemporary theological thinking from diverse perspectives, including liberation and feminist theologies.

Johannes Baptist Metz, *Poverty of Spirit* **(New York: Paulist Press, 1968).**
A poignant meditation on humility by an influential political theologian.

Henri Nouwen, *The Selfless Way of Christ: Downward Mobility and the Spiritual Life* **(Maryknoll, NY: Orbis Books, 2007).**
Nouwen's reflections on the counterintuitive, countercultural call to downward mobility in the Christian life.

INDEX